▶ ESSENTIAL SURVIVAL STORIES

FOREST AND JUNGLE SURVIVAL STORIES

BY ALEXIS BURLING

Essential Library

An Imprint of Abdo Publishing
abdobooks.com

ABDOBOOKS.COM

Published by Abdo Publishing, a division of ABDO, PO Box 398166, Minneapolis, Minnesota 55439. Copyright © 2024 by Abdo Consulting Group, Inc. International copyrights reserved in all countries. No part of this book may be reproduced in any form without written permission from the publisher. Essential Library™ is a trademark and logo of Abdo Publishing.

Printed in the United States of America, North Mankato, Minnesota.
102023
012024

THIS BOOK CONTAINS RECYCLED MATERIALS

Cover Photo: Jakub Maculewicz/Shutterstock Images
Interior Photos: Jakub Maculewicz/Shutterstock Images, 1; Curioso Photography/Shutterstock Images, 4–5; El Comercio/GDA/AP Images, 7; Red Line Editorial, 10; Shutterstock Images, 14–15, 18, 22, 38–39, 86–87, 91 (hat), 91 (boots), 91 (jacket), 91 (pocketknife, first aid), 91 (GPS), 91 (headlamp), 94; Henk Bogaard/Shutterstock Images, 17; R. P. Baiao/Shutterstock Images, 26–27; Vaclav Sebek/Shutterstock Images, 30; Dr. Morley Read/Shutterstock Images, 32; Anton Ivanov/Shutterstock Images, 35; AP Images, 36; The Asahi Shimbun/Getty Images, 43, 47; Eric Backman/Shutterstock Images, 48–49; Jess Kraft/Shutterstock Images, 51; Gary Gilardi/Shutterstock Images, 55; Randy Bjorklund/Shutterstock Images, 58; Todd Wells/AP Images, 60; Belikova Oksana/Shutterstock Images, 62–63; Emiliano Barbieri/Shutterstock Images, 66, 70; Michael Dodge/Getty Images Entertainment/Getty Images, 71; Jason Mintzer/Shutterstock Images, 73; Gilney Lima/Shutterstock Images, 74–75; Mia Zeus/iStockphoto, 78–79; Lars Bentrup/Shutterstock Images, 80; Bryan Berkowitz/Honolulu Star-Advertiser/AP Images, 82; Javier Cantellops/facebook.com/AmandaEllersMissing/AFP/Getty Images, 85; Cindy Hopkins/Alamy, 89; iStockphoto, 91 (map); Daphnusia Images/Shutterstock Images, 91 (bug spray); Peerasak Sapworasakun/Shutterstock Images, 91 (matches); Keith Homan/Shutterstock Images, 91 (filter); Osadcha Olga/Shutterstock Images, 97

Editor: Marie Pearson
Series Designer: Maggie Villaume

Library of Congress Control Number: 2023939430

PUBLISHER'S CATALOGING-IN-PUBLICATION DATA

Names: Burling, Alexis, author.
Title: Forest and jungle survival stories / by Alexis Burling
Description: Minneapolis, Minnesota: Abdo Publishing, 2024 | Series: Essential survival stories | Includes online resources and index.
Identifiers: ISBN 9781098292218 (lib. bdg.) | ISBN 9798384910152 (ebook)
Subjects: LCSH: Survival--Juvenile literature. | Adventure and adventurers--Juvenile literature. | Forests and forestry--Accidents--Juvenile literature. | Jungle survival--Juvenile literature. | Wilderness survival--Juvenile literature.
Classification: DDC 613.69--dc23

CONTENTS

CHAPTER ONE
PLUMMETING FROM THE SKY 4

CHAPTER TWO
DANGERS OF THE FOREST AND JUNGLE 14

CHAPTER THREE
A PATH OUT OF THE JUNGLE 26

CHAPTER FOUR
TWENTY-SEVEN YEARS IN HIDING 38

CHAPTER FIVE
A CAMPING TRIP GONE WRONG 48

CHAPTER SIX
LOST IN THE BOLIVIAN AMAZON 62

CHAPTER SEVEN
FOUND ALIVE AFTER 17 DAYS 74

CHAPTER EIGHT
SURVIVING THE FOREST AND JUNGLE 86

ESSENTIAL FACTS 100
GLOSSARY 102
ADDITIONAL RESOURCES 104
SOURCE NOTES 106
INDEX 110
ABOUT THE AUTHOR 112

The accounts in Chapters Six and Seven mention thoughts of suicide.

CHAPTER 1

PLUMMETING FROM THE SKY

It was December 24, 1971, and 17-year-old Juliane Koepcke couldn't wait to get out the door. She was headed from her part-time home in Lima, the capital city of Peru, to visit her father in Pucallpa, a small city located on the banks of the Ucayali River in the Amazon rainforest. It was the day before Christmas, one of Juliane's favorite holidays. She had just attended her high school graduation ceremony, and it was time to start celebrating.

Juliane's final destination was Panguana, a biological research station in the Peruvian jungle founded by her zoologist parents, Maria and

◀ The Amazon rainforest surrounds the Amazon River and the streams that flow into it.

Hans-Wilhelm Koepcke. At the time, it was a series of small, thatched cottages made out of wood and palm fronds. Located on the banks of the Río Yuyapichis, it is surrounded by untouched virgin forest. Juliane had lived there on and off for three years. She couldn't wait to spend more time surrounded by all the smells and sounds of the lush landscape and the fascinating creatures that called the Amazon rainforest their home.

When Juliane and her mother arrived at the Lima airport, it was packed with people. Some flights had been canceled, so there were few seats available. When the Koepckes were finally able to board LANSA Flight 508, which was a crowded, 86-passenger plane, they sat in the back on a three-seat bench, Juliane at the window and her mother beside her. It normally took less than an hour to get from Lima to Pucallpa by plane. Juliane figured she'd get some sleep during the flight.[1]

THE ORIGINS OF PANGUANA

The Panguana research station is the oldest biological research and conservation center in Peru. It is located on the banks of Río Yuyapichis, a tributary of the Río Pachitea, one of the main sources of the Amazon River.[2] It was founded in 1968 by German zoologists Maria and Hans-Wilhelm Koepcke. The couple wanted to study the creatures living in the lowland rainforest in the upper Amazon. The center's name was inspired by the local word for the undulated tinamou, a species of groundbird common to the Amazon River Basin.

▲ Juliane had just finished her schooling in Lima, Peru, when she boarded a plane on December 24, 1971.

LIGHTNING STRIKES

What was supposed to be a quick and easy trip across Peru soon turned into every traveler's worst nightmare. A few minutes after the flight attendants finished serving breakfast, Juliane's plane flew into a thunderstorm. Everything began to shake and shutter. Juliane and her mother closed their eyes, grabbed each other's hands, and squeezed hard.

"Suddenly, daylight turns to night and lightning flashes from all directions. People gasp as the plane shakes violently," Juliane recalled in an interview. "Bags, wrapped

LIGHTNING STRIKES ON AIRPLANES

The crash of LANSA Flight 508 was the deadliest lightning-strike disaster in aviation history. According to the National Weather Service, lightning strikes on passenger planes happen a couple of times a year.[5] Today, commercial planes are built to withstand lightning strikes. Airliners such as the Boeing 787 are designed so that the electrical current skims the outside of the plane and exits through the tail without affecting the aircraft's interior. Electrical parts around the fuel tank are also grounded to prevent explosions.

gifts, and clothing fall from overhead lockers. . . . People scream and cry."[3]

Juliane opened her eyes and watched in horror from her seat in the back row as a massive lightning bolt struck the plane's right wing. The plane began to nose-dive at breakneck speed. Suddenly, everything turned black. Juliane heard her mother say evenly, "Now it's all over."[4]

Then all Juliane heard was a deafening, all-encompassing silence. The plane had apparently split apart. The rupture had separated Juliane from everyone else around her. The next thing she knew, she was outside. Juliane was still strapped into her seat, but the seat had fallen away from the plane. When she looked around, all she could see was sky.

DEATH-DEFYING FREE FALL

From the moment LANSA Flight 508 started plummeting from the sky and Juliane became separated from the plane, she entered into a terrifying free fall. While still buckled in with her seatbelt, she fell more than 10,000 feet (3,000 m) from the sky—nearly two miles (3.2 km).[6] Her bench twirled in the air like a helicopter seed. Before Juliane blacked out, she remembered thinking that the treetops looked like broccoli.

When Juliane awoke on Christmas Day, she found herself underneath the bench, tangled up in dense foliage in the heart of the Peruvian Amazon. The minidress she was wearing was torn to shreds. From what she could tell, she was completely alone. "I will never forget the image I see when I open my eyes the next morning: The crowns of the giant trees above me are suffused with golden light, bathing everything in a green glow. I feel abandoned, helpless, and utterly alone. My mother's seat beside me is empty," she recalled.[7]

At that point, Juliane tried to stand up, but she couldn't support her weight. Her left eye was swollen shut and her right eye was badly bruised. But despite having fallen from such a high altitude, her injuries were relatively minor. She had a broken collarbone, a sprained knee, and several bloody gashes on her right shoulder. She had lost one of her shoes and her eyeglasses. Juliane was nearsighted and

▲ The plane carrying Juliane crashed before it reached Pucallpa. Pucallpa had the closest airport to Panguana.

needed her glasses to see anything that wasn't right in front of her face.

Exhausted and still afraid, Juliane lay there beneath the bench for the rest of the day and well into the next morning. It rained off and on the entire time, with huge droplets cascading down from the sky. She felt cold and was covered in dirt. Her clothes were soaked through from the downpours.

When she mustered enough strength to move, Juliane started crawling around on the ground. She needed to find out if her mother—or anyone else—had survived the crash. She screamed as loudly as she could, but all she heard were the familiar bird calls and buzzing insect sounds of the jungle.

Juliane had grown up exploring the Amazon, so she wasn't as frightened as someone else in her situation might have been. But she knew the territory was vast and sometimes impenetrable. There were endless steep and rocky ravines to fall down, wild pigs to steer clear of, and malaria-carrying mosquitoes to fight off. If she didn't find her way out soon, she might die. It was time to get moving and try to find civilization.

Given the severity of the crash, it was a miracle that Juliane was alive. But now she would have to use her survival skills and knowledge of the environment to traverse the Amazon without succumbing to disease, dehydration, starvation, or further injury. In her mind, she had many more years to live. She was determined to succeed so she could hug her father again.

SURVIVING IN THE WILDERNESS

In forest and jungle landscapes, getting stranded

THE AMAZON RAINFOREST

The Amazon is the largest rainforest in the world, covering about 40 percent of South America. It stretches across nine countries: Brazil, Peru, Guyana, Colombia, Ecuador, Bolivia, Suriname, French Guiana, and Venezuela. That's about the size of the lower 48 US states. The Amazon contains half of the world's tropical forest land. In 2020, it had two million square miles (5.2 million sq km) of original, undisturbed forest.[8]

without any means of help can be especially scary. Poisonous plants and insects are plentiful in these regions, and coming into contact with them can increase the risk of serious injury or death. With areas of thick foliage that can be easy to get lost in, steep terrain that is difficult to traverse, and high chances of flash floods, the odds of surviving such a harsh environment are poor, especially without adequate supplies.

But there are people who have done so and lived to tell the tale. In 1981, 22-year-old Yossi Ghinsberg joined a group of backpackers looking for gold deep in the Bolivian Amazon. After he got separated from his rafting partner and careened over a waterfall, he realized he was alone. For three weeks he wandered through the jungle trying to stay alive.

In May 2019, 35-year-old Amanda Eller decided to take a hike in the Makawao Forest Reserve on Hawaii's Maui island. She yearned for peace and quiet. But when she got lost after going off-trail, she spent the next 17 days fighting for her life in the forest.

Hiker Pamela Salant wanted nothing more than a little relaxation time when she and her boyfriend set out on a weekend trip in Oregon's Mount Hood National Forest in 2011. But when the couple separated to find a campsite,

Salant lost her bearings. She nearly lost her life after falling off a cliff.

According to survival expert Tim MacWelch, there are many reasons people get lost in the wilderness: difficult terrain, going off-trail, and accidents. The most important thing a person can do in such situations is to stay alert. "It's important to pay attention to your surroundings for many reasons. When we let our powers of observation lapse, we might step on a rattlesnake, walk right by a trail marker or take a wrong turn that would lead us into a dangerous place," he says. "The fix for this problem is to stay tuned in to your senses when you travel the wild. Listen and use your sense of smell to engage with the landscape. And use your vision most of all. When people hike with their head down, looking only at their feet and a few yards of trail ahead, they miss the beauty of nature—and the dangers as well."[9]

> **Sure, you can visit the wilderness to unplug and unwind, but you still need to keep your wits about you and pay attention to your surroundings.**[10]
>
> *—Tim MacWelch, writing for* Outdoor Life, *2021*

DANGERS OF THE FOREST AND JUNGLE

Jungles and other forests are often thought of as places full of fascinating flora and fauna. There, animals such as squirrels or ring-tailed lemurs scamper up trees while birds such as the harpy eagle soar through the sky. Piranhas, frogs, and other aquatic or amphibious creatures swim through muddy rivers and gushing streams. The terms *forest* and *jungle* are not interchangeable. A jungle is a type of forest that can be found only in certain parts of the world.

A forest is an ecosystem that's made up mostly of trees. Forests cover about one-third of Earth's land surface.[1] Scientists call forests the lungs of the planet

◀ It is easy to get turned around in the forest or jungle when wandering off the trail.

because they soak up carbon dioxide and release oxygen into the air.

Today, approximately 300 million people live in forests. More than one billion people depend on these areas for their livelihood.[2] Many more people visit forests to take part in recreational activities or to view the landscape's natural beauty. Scientists separate forests into three types based on latitude: boreal, temperate, and tropical. Tropical forests are also called rainforests.

Boreal forests, also called taigas, are one of the world's largest land biomes. They are located between 50 and 70 degrees latitude in Siberia, Scandinavia, and upper North America, including Canada and Alaska. Temperatures in boreal forests are often below freezing. Few plants and animals can survive there

LARGEST AND MOST BIODIVERSE FORESTS

The Amazon is the largest forest on the planet. It covers about 2.3 million square miles (6 million sq km) of northern South America. One in ten known wildlife species in the world live there. The Congo jungle in Africa is Earth's second-largest forest.[3] It stretches for more than 900,000 square miles (2.3 million sq km) throughout Cameroon, the Central African Republic, the Republic of the Congo, the Democratic Republic of the Congo, Equatorial Guinea, and Gabon.[4] The next three largest forests are the New Guinea rainforest, the Valdivian temperate rainforest in South America, and the Tongass National Forest in Southeast Alaska.

compared with more southerly forests. Conifers such as spruce, fir, and pine trees are the most common needle-leaf plant species throughout the taiga. Blueberry and cranberry bushes pepper the understory, providing food for birds and other animals. Moose roam the permafrost, the vast layer of soil that remains frozen throughout the year. Sometimes caribou roam across 1,700 square miles (4,400 sq km) to find food.[5]

Temperate forests are located along Earth's midlatitudes, so they have four distinct seasons—spring, summer, fall, and winter. In 2020, 16 percent of forests on the planet were temperate. There, annual temperatures have a wide range, from −22 to 86 degrees Fahrenheit (−30–30°C) depending

▼ It is important for the safety of both people and wildlife that anyone venturing into the woods keep a safe distance from wild animals.

▲ Bonobos eat fruit, leaves, flowers, and more in their jungle habitat.

on the season and where the forests are found on the globe. Most temperate forests receive an average of 30 to 59 inches (76–150 cm) of rain per year, though some can get up to 167 inches (424 cm) annually.[6]

Deciduous trees such as oaks, hickories, and maples thrive in temperate forests. These trees drop their leaves in the fall to save nutrients and energy during the winter. Bears, bobcats, squirrels, and deer populate the dense thickets in temperate forests. They hoard food, and some also hibernate during the chilly winter.

JUNGLES

The term *jungle* is often used interchangeably with *tropical rainforest*. Jungles can be found near the Tropics of Cancer and Capricorn. They cover large swaths of land in Southeast Asia, sub-Saharan Africa, South America, and Central America. Because of their location along the equator, jungles don't experience four seasons. The trees there are leafy and green all year round.

Jungles are the warmest and rainiest forests on Earth, with temperatures between 68 and 88 degrees Fahrenheit (20–31°C).[7] They get 79 to 394 inches (201–1,001 cm) of rain annually.[8] For jungles at low altitudes, temperatures hover around 95 degrees Fahrenheit (35°C) during the day with almost 100 percent humidity.[9] Sudden rainfall is always possible, as are frequent thunderstorms. The jungle's dry season, when it usually rains only once per day, runs from July through August. Monsoon season lasts from December through May. During this time, it rains almost constantly.

Though they make up less than 6 percent of the world's land surface area, jungles are home to more than 50 percent of Earth's plant and animal species.[10] The Amazon is the most biodiverse place on the planet. It has about 40,000 plant species, 3,000 freshwater fish species, and more than 370 reptile species.[11]

Jungles are unique places because their forests have many layers of foliage, each one with its own types of animals. Sometimes that specific layer is the sole place on the planet where a certain type of animal lives. For example, the Democratic Republic of the Congo is the only place in the world with bonobos. The red mangrove forest on the Panamanian island of Escudo de Veraguas is the only spot where visitors can see a pygmy three-toed sloth in the wild.

HAZARDOUS WEATHER

Many types of plants and animals have adapted to rich forest habitats and know what to do to survive. But for people, forests and jungles can also be dangerous. Getting stuck there without the proper gear can be a big challenge for anyone who is unprepared or undersupplied.

Weather conditions can turn rapidly in the forest, so it's best to always stay aware. Drought can cause extremely dry conditions that are ripe for fires. Wood debris on the forest floor increases the potential for larger wildfires to occur, especially when struck by a stray bolt of lightning. While fires can be catastrophic, small fires are good for the long-term health of the forest. They can even happen in damp rainforests, where small, natural fires burn the lower vegetation so new plants can grow. Weaker trees burn down while larger, sturdier trees usually survive.

On the other hand, human negligence is a big problem in forests throughout the world and a root cause of many fires. A discarded cigarette butt, a spark from a campfire, or a stray firecracker can strike some brush or a tree, causing it to ignite. All that small blaze needs is a gust of wind to turn it into a full-blown inferno. More than 73,000 wildfires burn an average of about 10,900 square miles (28,200 sq km) of land in the United States each year.[12]

THE EAGLE CREEK FIRE

In 2017, one of the deadliest wildfires in Oregon's history spread throughout the Columbia River Gorge, one of the state's most popular scenic areas. It was started by teenagers who were playing with fireworks along the Eagle Creek Trail during a fire ban. A 15-year-old boy threw a smoke bomb into a canyon, starting the blaze. The fire raged for months and burned more than 47,000 acres (19,020 ha) of forest—an area about the size of Washington, DC. The boy was ordered to pay $36.6 million in fines and was sentenced to 1,920 hours of community service and five years of probation.[13]

Flash floods from thunderstorms, tropical storms, or cyclones and typhoons are incredibly dangerous too. Just a few inches of fast-moving water can knock a human off-balance. Driving or walking through fast-moving water is never recommended. Hurricanes and tornadoes are a frequent risk in certain areas, such as Florida's national forests and its Everglades National Park.

DANGEROUS PLANTS AND ANIMALS

Forests are some of the most biodiverse places on Earth, but many of the animals and plants there can do serious harm to a human in extreme situations. Wild boars, cougars, jaguars, and bears are common throughout many forested areas.

▼ Bug spray can protect people in forests from being bitten by disease-carrying mosquitoes.

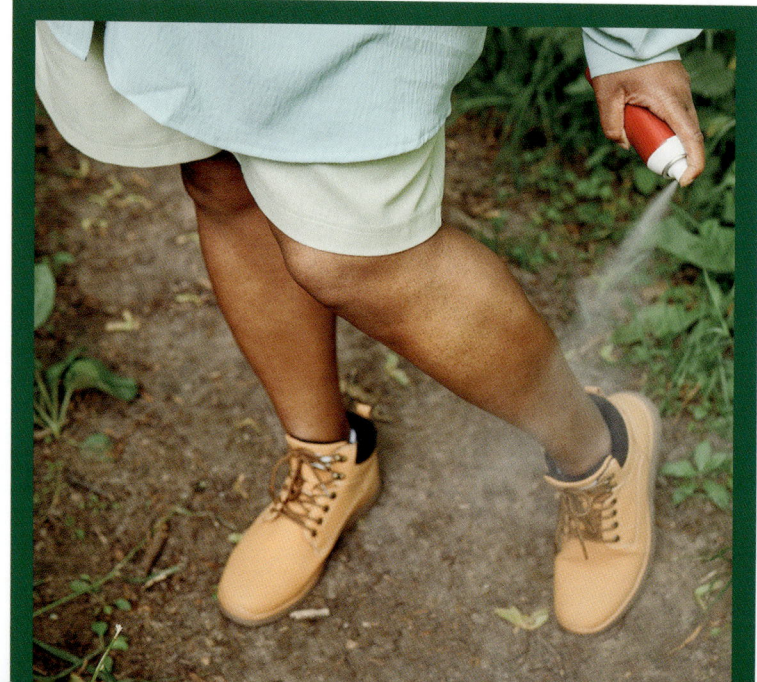

On their own, these animals are usually not dangerous if left alone, though some big cats have been known to stalk humans. But if provoked or cornered, they can attack people to defend themselves. Mothers are also protective of their young and will do whatever it takes to ensure their little ones stay safe.

Fish such as the electric eel and piranha are beautiful to look at, but while attacks on humans are rare, they can be lethal when they do happen. Electric eels send jolts of electricity through the water to stun prey. Piranhas are famous for their mighty jaws and sharp teeth.

One of the deadliest insects is the mosquito. In some areas, such as parts of South America and Africa, mosquitoes carry malaria, a disease that kills more than 600,000 people every year.[14] Mosquitoes in some areas are also carriers of dengue fever, a viral disease that causes a rash, a sometimes-fatal fever, and muscle pain. They also

> "Black piranhas and red-bellied piranhas are considered the most dangerous and aggressive toward humans.... For swimmers, the danger comes when the water level is low, prey is scarce, or you disturb its spawn buried in the riverbed—basically situations where the fish either feel really threatened or really hungry.[15]"
>
> —*Helen Thompson,* *Smithsonian Magazine, 2014*

carry yellow fever, which causes severe stomach pain and nausea, and West Nile fever, which causes headaches and muscle aches.

Venomous scorpions and spiders, as well as stinging fire ants and bullet ants, crawl through the forest. Snakes such as coral snakes, pit vipers, cobras, and anacondas slither up and down tree trunks, across plant leaves, and along the forest floor. The Brazilian wandering spider is the most venomous arachnid in the world. Its bite causes inflammation, shortness of breath, and even death if left untreated. The golden poison frog is an eye-catching but dangerous amphibian. It produces enough poison to kill ten humans.[16]

There are many edible plants in forests and jungles, but others are deadly if ingested or touched. Castor bean plants can grow up to 39 feet (12 m) tall. Their seeds are filled with a toxin called ricin. If even a small drop of ricin is ingested, it can kill a person in a few days.[17]

THE GYMPIE NETTLE

The gympie nettle plant grows in the jungles of northeast Australia and parts of Indonesia. Its green leaves are covered in tiny needlelike hairs that pierce the skin if touched. These spikes then secrete a toxin. People who have brushed up against gympie plants report severe pain and burning at the sting site that can last for days. Sometimes gympie hairs can become airborne. If inhaled, these fibers can severely harm the throat, esophagus, and lungs.

The strychnine tree is native to the rainforests of Southeast Asia and Australia. It has green leaves and bright-orange berries. If animals or humans eat a strychnine berry, the neurotoxin inside affects the central nervous system and has lethal effects. Forests and jungles also have some plants, such as poison ivy, that are not deadly but cause severe itching when touched.

ENVIRONMENTAL RISKS

In addition to steering clear of hazardous weather, plants, and animals, people who live in or spend time in forests or jungles need to pay attention to their surroundings. Falling trees can cause injury or death to explorers who walk or camp underneath them. Waterborne illnesses such as giardia are common risks that arise from drinking bacteria-contaminated water.

Perpetually wet conditions in jungles are another source of many visitors' problems. Damp, slippery rocks can cause dangerous falls. Constantly wet feet can lead to a brutal infection called trench foot. If left untreated, it can lead to gangrene or even require amputation. Preparing for these risks before a trip to the forest or jungle is key to avoiding problems that might come up.

CHAPTER 3

A PATH OUT OF THE JUNGLE

From the moment Juliane Koepcke realized she was stranded and completely alone in the Peruvian Amazon, she tried her best to focus. Though she couldn't see clearly, she assessed her surroundings and thought about what her parents would do in this situation. She knew they would tell her to remain calm, an important element of survival.

"Luckily, I'd lived in the jungle long enough as a child to be acquainted with the bugs and other creatures that scurry, rustle, whistle, and snarl," she recalled later. "There was almost nothing my parents hadn't taught me about the jungle. I only had to find this knowledge in my concussion-fogged head."[1]

◀ The Amazon rainforest is very large. Finding a stream or river and following it downstream can eventually lead to a human settlement.

GATHERING WATER IN THE JUNGLE

Unlike in the desert where water is scarce, collecting drinking water is one of the easiest parts of surviving in the jungle because it rains a lot. In addition, leaves in the rainforest tend to be larger than leaves in temperate or polar regions. The larger the leaf, the more sunlight it can take in, and the greater the surface area to collect rainwater and dew. Aside from rainwater, other sources of drinkable water in jungles include vines, palm tree stalks, and tree roots.

First, she identified the sounds and smells around her to get her bearings. She spotted sprinting ants, scurrying beetles, and jumping grasshoppers all over the ground and on the leaves of nearby plants. Massive trees towered overhead, their vines tangled up in the canopy. The constant buzzing of stingless bees and swarms of pesky mosquitoes filled the air, and a deep musty smell from decaying vegetation wafted up from the forest floor.

Next, she licked droplets of water off as many big leaves as she could reach to quench her thirst and listened for the sound of trickling water as she walked away from where she had landed after the plane crash. One of the most important lessons her parents had taught her about getting turned around in a forest was to find a stream or creek and then follow it because it might lead to a larger river, which would eventually lead to civilization. She soon stumbled upon a tiny spring, which turned into a stream. In between taking sips of water from the stream and sucking on a candy she found in a bag on the ground—the only thing edible she could find—she followed the stream to see where it would take her.

A GRUESOME DISCOVERY

Juliane walked for days. It was monsoon season, so it rained constantly. At night, the wood and brush were too damp to build a fire, so she huddled next to huge rocks and under large trees to stay dry. By the fourth day of her ordeal, December 28, the watch her grandmother had given her stopped working. She also missed her mother terribly.

During much of her journey, Juliane felt faint from hunger. There was hardly any fruit growing at that time of year, and without a knife, she couldn't cut into palm tree stems to reach their edible palm hearts. The lack of a fire meant she couldn't cook any fish. She knew most of the foliage around her would be poisonous, so she didn't dare eat any plant she didn't recognize.

Also on December 28, Juliane made a gruesome discovery. As she was walking, she heard the call of a king vulture. These large, white birds with black underwings and

🔺 King vultures live from southern Mexico to Argentina. They make their homes in dense tropical forests.

rainbow-colored necks appear and circle overhead when there's carrion on the ground. When she turned a bend in the stream, she saw one of the three-seat benches from LANSA Flight 508. A woman and two men, all deceased, were still strapped in. They had landed headfirst with such force that their upper bodies were jammed into the dirt. Their heads were underground, but their legs stuck straight up into the air.

"It was horrifying," Juliane recalled. "I didn't want to touch them, but I wanted to make sure that the woman wasn't my mother. I grabbed a stick and turned one of her feet carefully so I could see the toenails." When Juliane saw polish on the woman's nails, she gave a sigh of relief. "My mother never used polish on her nails."[2]

A BREAKTHROUGH

After seeing the wreckage, Juliane felt demoralized. She was weak from lack of nutrients and exhausted from the jungle slog. Her sunburned skin felt crisp to the touch. She knew she would have to find some sign of civilization if she was ever going to see her father again and figure out if her mother was still alive.

Then, the call of a bird gave her hope. On the fifth or sixth day of her journey—she was beginning to lose track of time—she heard the groaning and buzzing sound of a hoatzin, a chicken-sized bird with red eyes and a plume of orange feathers on its head. Hoatzins make their homes near open stretches of water, where people also tend to be. Juliane followed the noise until she came upon a clearing where the muddy river grew wide. However, there was no one in sight.

Juliane continued to follow the meandering river, hoping to come across something or someone who could help her. The riverbank was covered with thorny brush,

▲ The Amazon River looks brown because a lot of sediment, such as small pieces of soil and rock, gets swept up with the water.

and the heat of the day was so intense and the mosquitoes so fierce that she decided to swim instead. For the next five days, she swam in the middle of the river to steer clear of barb-tailed stingrays and biting piranhas, which prefer shallow water, and alligator-like reptiles called caimans, which bask on the shore.

> "The jungle is as much a part of me as my love for my husband, the music of the people who live along the Amazon and its tributaries, and the scars that remain from the plane crash.[3]"
>
> —Juliane Koepcke in an interview with the New York Times, June 18, 2021

By the tenth day, Juliane was so frail and exhausted that all she could do was float in the water. Occasionally she knocked against a drifting log and bruised her arm or leg. Fish nibbled on her skin underneath the surface. As she stared up at the sky, she tried to relax and let the slow current take her downstream.

PEOPLE!

It was late afternoon, and Juliane was looking to bed down for the night when she saw a large boat. Beyond the boat there was a rugged dirt path that led into the jungle. Though she could hardly stand up, she dragged herself out of the water to follow the path into a dense thicket. There, at the end of the path, was a small hut with a palm leaf roof.

Juliane nearly collapsed with joy. Inside the hut, she found a container of gasoline. The gash in her arm was covered in maggots that had burrowed deep beneath her skin. She poured the gasoline onto the wound thinking it would force the bugs to evacuate the site. It didn't work. "The pain was intense as the maggots tried to get further into the wound," she remembered. "I pulled out about 30 maggots and was very proud of myself."[4]

Tired of sleeping in the dirt, Juliane spent the night and most of the following afternoon resting in the hut. The next evening, on January 3, 1972, she awoke from a nap to hear the sound of voices. She rushed outside to find a group of Peruvian

MYIASIS MISERY

During her trek out of the jungle, Juliane Koepcke developed a case of myiasis, when fly larvae burrow under the skin. This can happen in many ways. A fly can lay eggs on a wound or attach its eggs to a mosquito, which then bites people. When these eggs hatch, the larvae crawl underneath the skin. Myiasis occurs frequently in tropical and subtropical areas, including Central America, South America, Africa, and the Caribbean islands. The condition is treated by having a doctor manually remove the larvae or maggots from the area. Though pouring gasoline on a wound was a common solution in the 1970s, using oil, kerosene, or lighter fluid is now considered unsafe because it can burn or infect the skin.

▲ Indigenous societies have lived along the Amazon River for thousands of years. They fish in the river and use it for transportation.

fishermen and forestry workers, who were shocked to see the dirty, emaciated girl emerge. "I'm a girl who was in the LANSA crash," she said to them in Spanish. "My name is Juliane."[5]

The men fed Juliane and treated her wounds. The next day, they took her in a boat back to the nearest village, where she was flown back to Pucallpa. A day later, she finally got to hug her father.

Ninety-one people died in the crash of LANSA Flight 508, including Juliane's mother.[6] Juliane was the only survivor. In 1998, German filmmaker Werner Herzog made

▲ Juliane received letters from around the world after her rescue.

a documentary about her fall from the sky, called *Wings of Hope*. In 2011, Juliane wrote a book about her experience titled *When I Fell from the Sky: The True Story of One Woman's Miraculous Survival*.

Over time, Juliane married and became a biologist and librarian at the Bavarian State Collection of Zoology in Munich, Germany. She also took over as director of Panguana and traveled there regularly. The nature reserve covers 4,000 acres (1,620 ha) and has more than 500 species of trees, 160 species of reptiles and amphibians, 100 species of fish, 600 species of butterflies, and 380 species of birds.[7]

Scientists use it to research biodiversity. "On my lonely 11-day hike back to civilization, I made myself a promise," Juliane said. "I vowed that if I stayed alive, I would devote my life to a meaningful cause that served nature and humanity."[8]

Juliane has also partnered with neighboring Indigenous communities to make more jobs available and has helped pay for the construction of a new school. "Just to have helped people and to have done something for nature means it was good that I was allowed to survive," she told the *New York Times* in 2021.[9]

CHILDREN SURVIVE THE AMAZON

On May 1, 2023, a small plane carrying seven people crashed in the Colombian Amazon. The passengers included a mother and her four children, ranging from one to 13 years old. When the mother died four days after the crash, only the children survived. They belonged to the Witoto Indigenous group, and they used their traditional knowledge of the jungle to stay alive and find fruit safe to eat. The oldest sibling made shelters by using hair ties to hold branches together. Hundreds of Colombian army troops and Indigenous volunteers searched for the children. Search and rescue dogs found them on June 9, 40 days after the crash. The children were hungry, but all were alive.

CHAPTER 4

TWENTY-SEVEN YEARS IN HIDING

In December 1941, World War II (1939–1945) gripped all corners of the globe. The world was split into two major camps. The Allied powers—the United Kingdom, France, Russia, and China—were on one side, and the Axis powers—Germany, Italy, and Japan—were on the other. The Allies were trying to put a stop to the spread of fascism, halt Japanese expansion, and prevent German dictator Adolf Hitler and his Nazi Party from expanding their empire across the world.

On December 7, 1941, the Japanese military launched a surprise attack on the US naval base in Pearl Harbor, Hawaii, in retaliation for the United States'

◀ Approximately 47 percent of Guam's land is forested. Native species include fruit bats and eight-spot butterflies.

restrictions on transporting oil and other goods to Japan and freezing all Japanese financial assets in US banks. The bombing killed 2,403 Americans—2,008 sailors, 218 soldiers, 109 marines, and 68 civilians.[1] The next day, the United States joined World War II on the side of the Allies.

December 8 was a historic day too. That morning, the Japanese invaded Guam, a 210-square-mile (544 sq km) island and US territory in the western Pacific about the size of Chicago, Illinois.[2] After a two-day battle, the Japanese forces won control of the island. They maintained their hold on Guam for almost three years. But in July 1944, the United States returned to reclaim what it had lost.

On July 21, 1944, US troops landed in Guam to retake it. Although Japan surrendered in the Battle of Guam on August 10, more than 1,000 Japanese soldiers

JAPANESE OCCUPATION OF GUAM

After the Japanese took control of Guam in 1941, they ran the island by force. Japanese troops rounded up the native Chamorros and put them to work in Japanese military buildings. About 10 percent of the native islanders were killed for disobeying orders. In 1944, the United States reclaimed Guam, and the Japanese occupiers fled. But over the years, time has allowed some old wounds to heal. In 2019, more than 600,000 Japanese tourists visited the island.[3] One of the most popular sites to visit is a reconstruction of the shelter that Shoichi Yokoi dug into the jungle floor.

fled in small groups into the hilly jungle.[4] The Allies had captured or killed many of these holdouts by the time World War II ended in 1945, but about 130 remained in hiding.[5] Most knew World War II was over because of leaflets the US Army dropped into the jungle. Still, they refused to turn themselves in because of their allegiance to their country. One of them was Shoichi Yokoi.

DEEP IN HIDING

> ### GUAM'S DIVERSE WILDLIFE
>
> As an island in the Pacific Ocean, Guam is isolated from large landmasses. Still, it is home to an array of flora and fauna, especially in its forested areas. There, water buffalos lounge in rushing streams to escape the heat of the day. Geckos, blue-tailed skinks, and chameleons scurry up and down trees while rose-crowned fruit doves, kingfishers, and the rare Guam rail fly through the sky. One invasive species is the venomous brown tree snake, which is killing off much of the bird population on the island. In 2017, there were more than two million brown tree snakes in Guam.[6]

The northern half of Guam is mostly flat and made up of coral reefs, woods, urban areas, and farmland. The southern half is volcanic in origin, with rolling hills, grassy landscapes, and plenty of waterways. But throughout its interior, much of the island is forested. In fact, approximately half of it consists of lush jungle landscape. After the Japanese were routed from Guam, Yokoi and a group of about nine or ten others did their best to survive by staying together and adapting to their environment. "From the outset they took enormous care not to be detected, erasing their footprints as they moved through the undergrowth," Yokoi's nephew, Omi Hatashin, told BBC News years later.[7]

For the first few years, Yokoi and his crew sneaked into locals' pastures at night and killed cattle to eat. Eventually, as they moved farther inland along the Talofofo River basin, they ate whatever they could find in the forest. They picked coconuts out of towering trees, foraged for papayas, and fished out frogs and eels from the streams. When food was scarce, they clobbered rats over the head and ate their flesh raw. Most of the time, they lived inside caves to stay warm and sheltered from the rain.

Eking out an existence while remaining undiscovered was difficult. Before long, most of Yokoi's group aside from Yokoi and two others were captured, had died from illness, or had surrendered. Yet Yokoi continued. He dug out a massive tunnel underground and constructed a cave that was resistant to flooding. He covered the entrance with a camouflaged mat he wove out of bamboo stalks.

To hunt for food, Yokoi made traps to catch river shrimp and field mice. He learned how to remove the poisonous glands of cane toads so he could eat them without becoming infected. He boiled water to kill any parasites. Eventually, he brought the toads into his cave in order to deal with a cockroach infestation. When it came time to make a fire underground, he used coconut husks to filter out the smoke so his whereabouts wouldn't be detected.

When Yokoi's uniform deteriorated because of Guam's tropical heat and humidity, he put his background as a tailor

▼ People later visited Yokoi's cave, though it eventually collapsed.

to good use. He ripped off pieces of tree bark and spun the tiny strips into thread. He then used that thread to weave a type of cloth similar to bark cloth or burlap. From there, he made sets of shirts and pants with pockets, belt loops, and buttonholes that would protect him from the sun and swarming mosquitoes.

The entire process took many months to complete. But because Yokoi had so much free time, he welcomed the job. "It might actually have been good for my mental condition to keep myself thoroughly occupied with day-to-day business," he wrote in a memoir. "I derived simple delight and satisfaction from every moment of these activities."[8]

Yokoi lived like that for 20 years, mostly alone but occasionally in the company of his two original army buddies. He nearly perished three times because of sickness. In 1964, the two other Japanese holdouts

YOKOI'S UNDERGROUND LAIR

Yokoi's underground home was remarkably complex. It was three feet (0.9 m) high, nine feet (2.7 m) long, and located seven feet (2.1 m) underground.[9] The walls and floor were lined with strong canes of bamboo to prevent anything from caving in. At the entrance, a handmade ladder extended into the cave's depths. The structure took three months to build. It even had an indoor toilet with a hole so waste could flow into the underground river below.

mysteriously died. Some historians say the men drowned in a flood. A medical examiner stated they were poisoned, likely when they ate toxic cycad nuts. Whatever the cause, Yokoi lived in total isolation in the jungle for the next eight years.

FOUND!

On January 24, 1972, two native Chamorro men—Jesus M. Duenas and Manuel D. Garcia—were out fishing when they spotted a mysterious man lurking by the river about four miles (6.4 km) from the small village of Talofofo. When they tried to approach him to see who he was, the man lunged at them as if to attack them. Duenas and Garcia quickly subdued the man and tied his hands behind his back. They brought him to Hagåtña, Guam, a larger city ten miles (16 km) away, where he was questioned by authorities.[10]

What the Hagåtña authorities were amazed to discover was that the man in front of them, Shoichi Yokoi, was a Japanese holdout who had fought in World War II and had been hiding in the jungle for nearly 28 years. At the time of his capture, Yokoi was 56 years old and weighed less than 90 pounds (41 kg).[11] He wore a straggly beard, was missing several teeth, had deep calluses on his fingers, and had tanned and wrinkled skin from constant sun exposure. Still, doctors thought he was in remarkable shape given the circumstances.

News of Yokoi's reemergence from the Guam jungle quickly spread. People around the world were shocked and amazed that one man could survive for so long on his own in such an unforgiving environment. A few weeks after his capture, following his recovery at Guam Memorial Hospital, Yokoi was flown back to Japan on a chartered jet. When he saw Mount Fuji, one of Japan's great symbols of beauty, he burst into tears.

> Your Majesties, I have returned home. I deeply regret that I could not serve you well. The world has certainly changed, but my determination to serve you will never change.[14]
>
> —Shoichi Yokoi, during a visit to the Imperial Palace, where Japan's emperor and empress lived, in 1972

A massive ceremony was held at Tokyo's airport to welcome Yokoi home. More than 5,000 people attended.[12] An additional 70 million watched on television.[13] People across Japan and the world considered Yokoi to be a national hero.

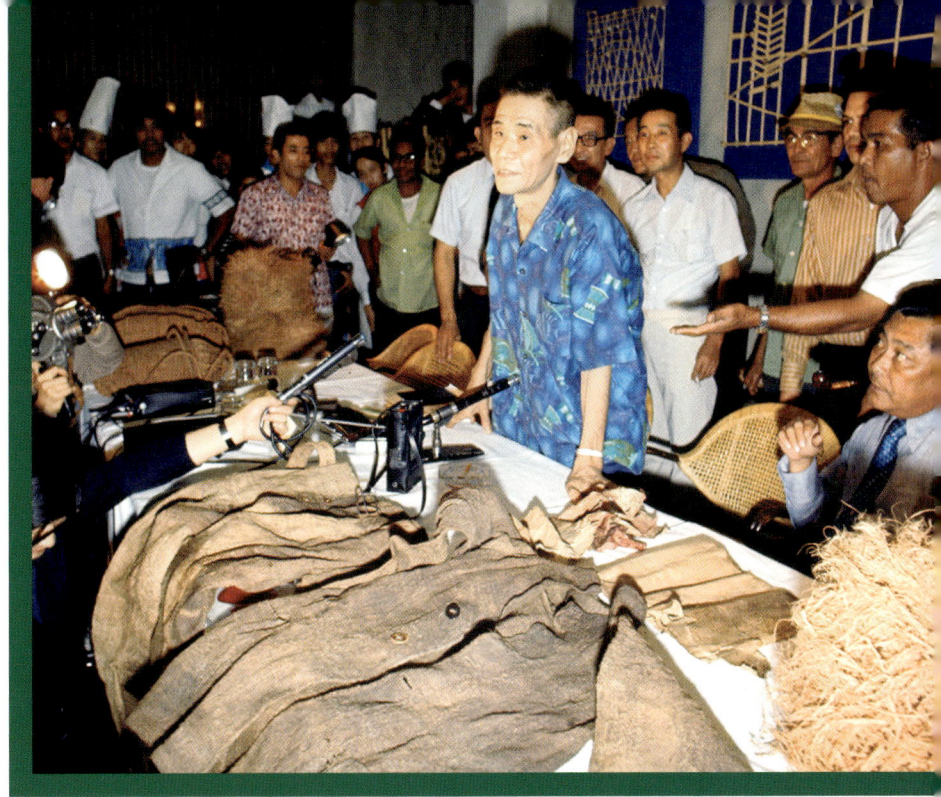

▲ Yokoi was interviewed many times after he was discovered, including about the clothes he made.

In the years following his return to his native country, Yokoi did his best to assimilate into society. In November 1972, he moved back to his hometown of Nagoya and got married. Two years later, he wrote a best-selling book about his experiences and ran for a position in the Japanese parliament but didn't win. He returned a few times to Guam.

On September 22, 1997, Yokoi died from a heart attack. He was 82 years old. In 2009, Yokoi's book, *Private Yokoi's War and Life on Guam, 1944–1972*, was published in English. The cave where he lived for so many years is still marked on tourist maps.

CHAPTER 5

A CAMPING TRIP
GONE WRONG

It was a beautiful July day in the summer of 2011. Twenty-eight-year-old preschool teacher Pamela Salant and her boyfriend, 31-year-old Aric Essig, were heading out for a quick weekend camping trip. They liked to go camping often, and this time they had chosen to go to Mount Hood National Forest, a 1,700-square-mile (4,400 sq km) area in Oregon that includes temperate rainforest and pine forest.[1]

Salant and Essig drove from their home in Portland, Oregon, to the trailhead for Bear Lake, a small reservoir. According to the trail book, the hike to the destination would take only about an hour without much elevation gain, so it was not too strenuous.

◀ Mount Hood is a volcano in the Cascade Range. It is Oregon's highest mountain.

MOUNT HOOD NATIONAL FOREST

Mount Hood National Forest is a tree-filled region that stretches south from the Columbia River Gorge across miles of forested mountains, lakes, and streams. It has eight distinct wilderness areas, all flanked around the dormant volcano that is Mount Hood. On one side of the mountain, there is a temperate rainforest full of towering Douglas fir trees. On the other, a dry forest full of Ponderosa pine trees receives much less rainfall. More than four million people explore the area each year.[2] Visitors can hike, bike, kayak, swim, fish, ski, and pick berries or mushrooms throughout the park.

They planned to hike back out on Sunday morning.

The excursion didn't go according to plan. By the time Salant and Essig got to the lake at about one o'clock in the afternoon, the air was filled with tension. They had been arguing much of the way up the trail. When the couple got to the end of the trail, they set down their tent and backpacks filled with their water purifier, cooking equipment, food, and sleeping bags at a campsite but then had another argument about whether the spot was private enough. They decided to look for a site on the other side of the lake. Salant stalked off in one direction, thinking a walk on her own would help her calm down. Essig followed the trail in the other direction.

Salant was supposed to meet Essig on the western end of the lake. But when Essig made it to the other side, his girlfriend wasn't there. An hour passed. Then two hours

⚠ Approximately one-third of Mount Hood National Forest is designated as wilderness, meaning no permanent roads or buildings can be constructed and people cannot be long-term residents there.

went by. Salant still hadn't shown up. At first, Essig felt annoyed. But at the six-hour mark, Essig's irritation had turned into worry. He wondered if she was talking to other campers she met along the way or if something terrible had happened to her.

A BRUTAL FALL

What Essig didn't know at the time was that soon after he and Salant separated, Salant had gone off the trail to get around parts of the lake where the underbrush was too thick on the shore, and she had gotten lost. Worse, Salant hadn't taken along any of the supplies in her backpack, such as a compass, map, flashlight, phone, or drinking water. She was wearing only a tank top, shorts, socks, and boots.

The longer Salant hiked to find her way back to Bear Lake, the more lost she became. She tried to backtrack down through a drainage basin and up over a pile of rocks to catch her bearings. But instead of the lake she thought would be there when she arrived at the top, there was a view of a snowcapped peak in the distance. The sun had started to go down and daylight was growing dimmer; she'd been hiking for more than six hours since leaving Essig. Feeling frantic, she screamed his name but got no response.

Salant scrambled up and down a few rocky, tree-lined ridges and then spotted another lake below. Even if it wasn't Bear Lake, she thought there would probably be people camping there who might be able to help her. She sped up, not wanting to get caught without shelter in the dark. But as she was making her way down a rocky ridge, she tripped and fell nearly 50 feet (15 m) to the ground below.[3]

> **WILDERNESS FIRST AID**
>
> A broken leg or other serious injury in the wilderness requires medical intervention by trained professionals. But there are some plants that can be used in emergency situations until help arrives. Greta de la Montagne, a holistic health practitioner with the American Herbalist Guild, suggests wrapping a wound in burdock leaves to protect against germs. With its clusters of tiny white flowers, common yarrow can be applied directly to wounds and burns to ease the pain. Grown throughout North America, old man's beard—also called beard lichen—is an antimicrobial. When soaked in water, it's used to fight bacterial infections.

Injured and alone, Salant spent the night at the bottom of a cliff, though she didn't realize yet how badly she was injured. When she woke up the next morning, it looked as though her left leg was broken or at least fractured, with a jagged bone projecting outward through her skin. Her right leg was covered in dirt and blood. "All right," Salant said to herself. "I need to get to water. I'm thirsty, and I need to clean up this cut."[4]

Eventually, Salant found a stream about a quarter of a mile (0.4 km) away.[5] Because she was in excruciating pain, it took her an hour to get there by scooting along on her bottom in a three-limbed crab walk. The process was brutal. But when she finally arrived, the icy cool water quenched her thirst and eased some of the pain of her injury.

LEAP INTO THE BEYOND

Salant's attempts to find a water source helped her stay hydrated in the hot sun. But the stream was helpful in another way. Salant knew that small streams flow into larger ones. Because she had looked at a map before the hike, she knew that this stream would lead to the Columbia River. If she followed the water source, she would eventually find civilization.

There was only one problem. The stream Salant had stumbled upon was Lindsey Creek. It did eventually flow into the Columbia. But first it gushed and surged through a series of majestic but steep waterfalls and into a deep gorge—something Salant hadn't realized when looking at the map. Not long into her journey of hopping across fallen logs and crawling along the craggy shore, Salant encountered a steep ravine. It was too difficult to turn around and go back the

▲ Harrison Falls is just one of the waterfalls along Lindsey Creek. It can't be seen from the trail.

way she had come. Crossing the churning stream with her broken leg was too dangerous. Staying where she was under a canopy of trees with no trail in sight would mean she might never be found.

Before she could change her mind, Salant stood up on one leg and pushed herself off the ledge. She jumped 12 feet (3.7 m) into the shallow pool below. "I can't believe I'm doing this!" she yelled right before she took the leap.[6]

When she landed, Salant fell over to one side and got soaked in the water. But aside from getting wet, she survived the fall without further injury. Suddenly, she heard the sound of a helicopter overhead, but the area where she had landed was too covered in trees for anyone to see her from above. The helicopter flew away.

It was getting late, and she'd been on the move all day, so Salant found a flat area where she could get some rest. She covered herself in strips of moss to keep warm. She took out the built-in bra in her tank top

> "That drive to live was so strong for me, and I just like really felt like I just wasn't done yet. I never wanted to give up really, I just was not certain my body could handle it with my broken leg.[7]"
>
> —Pamela Salant, reflecting on her experience lost in the Mount Hood wilderness, 2011

and put it over her head to seal in heat from her head. Then she tried not to worry too much about cougars or bears and drifted off to sleep.

A MIRACULOUS RESCUE

For the next two days, Salant followed the river, hoping she would come across a trail or some hikers. That didn't happen. She thought of Essig and the rest of her friends and family and wondered if she'd ever see them again. She washed out her wounds repeatedly and wrapped the injured part of her leg in her underwear to protect it from dirt and debris. She tried suturing her leg with thorns from a nearby bush, but it was too prickly and painful to endure.

Starving, Salant also couldn't stop thinking about food. She tried to eat a caterpillar and a slug, but both were so gooey and slimy that she couldn't bring herself to swallow. She knew Mount Hood was known for salmonberries that were edible, so when she came upon a bush, she stuffed as many as she could into her mouth.

On the morning of the fourth day, Salant had finally reached her breaking point. "I've had enough of this," she said to herself. "I'm going to be found today. Or I'm going to die. But the journey is coming to an end."[8]

▲ Salmonberries look similar to raspberries. They can be yellow, orange, or red, and the shrub they grow on stands three to 12 feet (0.9–3.7 m) tall.

That morning and through the afternoon, she tried to get herself to a dry place that was visible from the sky. She heard the motor of a helicopter overhead sometime in the late morning. She waved her arms in the air and yelled as loudly as she could, hoping they would see her. Later that afternoon, when she was scrounging again for something to eat, she heard movement in the trees behind her. She was crawling to another salmonberry bush when she heard a voice: "You must be Pam."[9]

She later learned that Essig had used his cell phone to call for help when she didn't arrive at the other end of the lake. A search and rescue effort began, and crews had been looking for Salant since then. On August 2, the day she was rescued and nearly 96 hours since she and Essig had started the hike, four members of a volunteer alpine rescue team called the Hood River Crag Rats had spent the morning descending Lindsey Creek. They had been in radio contact with the Oregon Army National Guard helicopter that had seen Salant waving her arms from above.

THE HOOD RIVER CRAG RATS

The Hood River Crag Rats are just one of many search and rescue teams all over the world that work to save people who get stranded in the wilderness. Formed in 1926, the Crag Rats are the oldest mountain rescue organization in the United States. Members of the all-volunteer crew scale glaciers, tread across ice-strewn cliffs, rappel down waterfalls, and descend into ravines to extract injured hikers from treacherous areas in forests throughout Mount Hood National Forest and the Columbia River Gorge in Oregon and Washington.

A little while later, a medevac chopper arrived. There was no place for the helicopter to land because massive Douglas fir trees surrounded the stream. So while the helicopter hovered above, flight medic Ben Sjullie lowered down from a pulley into an area the size of a small SUV. Ten minutes later, Salant was hanging from a cable wrapped up in Sjullie's arms. For the first time since she left Essig standing there at Bear Lake, she broke into tears.

"I just don't know if she could have made it past the point [where] we'd found her," says Tom Scully of the

▲ The Crag Rats conduct rescues in both summer and winter and are skilled in rock climbing and in avalanche rescues.

Crag Rats. "[That was] one of the burliest hikes I've ever been on. It wasn't even a hike. It was survival. There's nothing out there but nothing. We were all soaked and scraped up. And she had been at this for days without gear or clothes. She's amazing."[10]

Salant was transported to Legacy Emanuel Medical Center in Portland and stayed there for a week. Her parents and other family members flew out from Boston to make sure she was all right. In addition to the gash on her right leg and the severe fracture just below her left knee, she had compression fractures in her spine and wounds, cuts, and bruises all over her body. But she was just thankful to be alive.

When Salant's injuries were mostly healed and she stopped using crutches, she and Essig went camping again. Her friends couldn't believe it. But she wanted to prove her love for nature hadn't been erased just because of her trauma. "Are you kidding?" Salant said when they asked her if it was wise to go camping again so soon. "It's all I want to do."[11]

CHAPTER 6

LOST IN THE BOLIVIAN
AMAZON

In November 1981, 22-year-old Yossi Ghinsberg was ready for something new. He had just finished up a stint in the Israel Defense Forces and had three years in the navy under his belt. He needed a change of pace before deciding what his next step in life would be.

Ever since he had read a book set in the Amazon jungle as a teenager, Ghinsberg had wanted to explore the legendary environment, so he flew to South America. He figured he would work out a plan when he got there. He aimed to travel by carrying the few belongings he brought with him in his backpack. When he wasn't camping, he would stay in youth

◀ Ghinsberg spent time in La Paz, Bolivia. La Paz is the capital city of Bolivia and is located on the western side of the country.

hostels, which are cheap dormitory-style inns with rooms that are shared with other people.

First, Ghinsberg hitchhiked from Venezuela to Colombia and then on to Bolivia. Along the way he met Marcus Stamm, a backpacker from Switzerland who was also interested in seeing the Amazon. The two decided to travel together to La Paz, Bolivia. In La Paz, they met two more backpackers: Kevin Gale, an American photographer from Oregon, and Karl Ruprechter, an Austrian who said he was a geologist. By late November, Ruprechter had persuaded the other three to join him on a multiweek trek into the Bolivian Amazon to find a remote village inhabited by Indigenous Tacanan people. There, Ruprechter insisted, they would find gold, a prospect which excited the other three.

From La Paz, the foursome flew north in a small plane to the town of Apolo. From there, they took a small riverboat chartered by locals down the Tuichi River. The boat's destination was Asariamas, a village north of Apolo at the intersection of the Tuichi and Asariamas Rivers. When the boat arrived, the group was full of excitement about the prospect of further adventures. But little did they know that their journey would be far from the fun trip they had dreamed about.

A DISASTROUS TREK

Before Ghinsberg, Stamm, Gale, and Ruprechter embarked on their trek into the Bolivian Amazon in an area that is now Madidi National Park, they asked the people in Asariamas about how to prepare for their journey. The locals warned them that the hike would be very difficult and probably unwise. But the four decided to take the risk anyway. They packed up some rice, beans, water, and other supplies and headed out into the dense, humid jungle on foot. A few days into their hike, they had already run out of food.

"We were constantly hungry. We would walk long days, having eaten nothing at all," said Ghinsberg. "We shot at monkeys and ate them. I would have put anything in my mouth."[1]

MADIDI NATIONAL PARK

Ghinsberg began his journey in 1981 in part of the Bolivian Amazon. Today, that area of the jungle is known as Madidi National Park. It became a protected conservation area and national park in 1995. Madidi covers an area of 7,320 square miles (18,958 sq km) and is full of giant cliffs, lush cloud forest, and meandering waterways. The park is home to 204 species of reptiles; 213 species of amphibians; 272 species of mammals, including jaguars and howler monkeys; 496 species of fish; 1,254 species of birds, including vibrant macaws; and more than 120,000 species of insects.[2] People from six different tribes live in 46 Indigenous communities spread out over the area.[3]

▲ Capuchins are among the monkeys that live in the Bolivian Amazon.

In addition, Stamm had developed trench foot and couldn't keep up with the others because his feet were always in pain. After several days of travel, they also hadn't found the remote village. They decided to abandon their original on-land plan and returned to Asariamas. There, the locals helped them build a raft, which the four then navigated down the Tuichi River. Ruprechter's new plan was to head to a small gold quarry called Curiplaya. From there, they would row downstream to a village called Rurrenabaque near the Beni River then go back to La Paz.

Even that idea didn't go according to plan. At the meeting of the Tuichi and Ipurama Rivers, Ruprechter refused to continue, claiming the water would become too choppy around the San Pedro Canyon, and he couldn't swim. After many arguments, the group split up. Ghinsberg and Gale would continue on in the water until they got to the San Pedro waterfall, walk around the waterfall, and then raft downriver. Ruprechter and Stamm decided to set out on foot up the Ipurama River to Ipurama village. Their plan was to return to Apolo and reunite with Ghinsberg and Gale in La Paz by Christmas.

SURVIVAL

Ghinsberg and Gale's rafting expedition down the Ipurama River and through the San Pedro Canyon was disastrous from the start. Almost immediately after they set off, they realized the rapids were too choppy. As they careened toward the San Pedro falls, Gale managed to get safely to shore, though his feet got bruised in the tumble of the roiling water. Then he looked up in horror to see Ghinsberg still heading for the waterfall. He tried to swim out to him, but the current was too strong, and he was forced to turn back. Ghinsberg hurtled over the cliff into the deep gorge below.

"It was a rollercoaster ride which lasted for 15 or 20 minutes. It was all I could do to keep my head above water,"

SAVED FROM DROWNING

Kevin Gale watched Yossi Ghinsberg hurtle over the massive waterfall in the San Pedro Canyon. But after Gale managed to swim to shore, he spent days by himself in the jungle, looking for Ghinsberg. He survived by hunting small animals with his machete and eating eggs from nests. His feet were covered in bloody, oozing sores, and he could barely stand, so he decided to float down the river on a broken tree trunk in the hope that someone would see him. A while later, two Indigenous people spotted him in the churning water. He screamed to them, asking for help in Spanish. They took hold of the tree trunk, pulling Gale to shore.

Ghinsberg recalled later. "When I finally arrived on the shore, I had a moment of complete exhilaration that I had survived. A few seconds later came the first feeling of disaster and despair. Even then, I thought it would only be a few hours until we connected again."[4]

Ghinsberg didn't drown in the waterfall or break any bones. But he was in a perilous situation. He called out to Gale, but the sound of the thunderous falls was too overpowering. There was no way to climb back up the steep ravine. He was stranded in the middle of the jungle without any way to get help, without any idea of where he was, and without enough supplies. Luckily, he still had his backpack.

For the next three weeks, he tried his best to survive in the jungle. He lived off berries and whatever other fruit he could find. He foraged for eggs in birds' nests, collected rainwater in leaves, and drank water from streams. He fended off attacks from wild boars and tried to steer clear of venomous snakes. One night, he defended himself against a jaguar by igniting the gas from a can of mosquito repellent with a lighter—a trick he copied from a James Bond movie.

Ghinsberg was still alive, but his body was battered and bruised—especially his feet. After all the hiking and near-constant rain, the skin had torn away from his soles, leaving them bloody and infected. He mistakenly spent a night in a termites' nest and woke up with bites all over his body. He impaled himself on a stick after sliding down a ravine. He even discovered that worms had burrowed under his skin.

The nights were the worst. The thick canopy blotted out the moon and starlight, so it was pitch-black. The jungle echoed with the calls of wild animals. He had little with which to protect himself and worried constantly about being attacked.

On the nineteenth day, Ghinsberg almost drowned when he fell into a mud pit after a rainstorm. He thought of just letting himself sink into the muck and die. But a sliver of strength came to him, and he dragged himself out of

▲ The Beni River flows through what is now Madidi National Park. Eventually it joins with another river to form the Madeira River, which makes part of the border between Bolivia and Brazil.

the bog. He decided he had been struggling too long to give up now.

RESCUED IN THE NICK OF TIME

After nearly three weeks of struggle in the Amazon jungle, Ghinsberg was deflated and gaunt. But on the twentieth day, he heard the rumble of an engine. Thinking he was hallucinating, he made his way to the nearest river to check out the commotion. To his surprise, Gale appeared with a group of Indigenous people from San José de Uchupiamonas, a remote town located about five hours away from Rurrenabaque by boat. After Gale had been separated from Ghinsberg, he had searched for his friend but never found him. Five days later—weak and nearly delirious—he was found by two Indigenous villagers. He told them what had happened, and they had organized a search and rescue mission. Led by Don Tico Tuvela Rivera,

▼ Ghinsberg, *left*, poses with film director Greg McLean. McLean directed the film *Jungle* based on Ghinsberg's experience.

> **I became a very simple person. The simple things are the most precious to me. I don't ascribe much significance to the things I have now. That feeling of touching death has never left me.**[5]
>
> —Yossi Ghinsberg, looking back on his perilous journey in the Amazon, 2016

the crew had been searching for Ghinsberg since then.

Gale and the rest of the crew loaded Ghinsberg into a boat, and they sailed down the river to the closest medical facility. Ghinsberg spent three months recovering in San José de Uchupiamonas before he could walk again. In 1985, he wrote a book about his near-death journey called *Back from Tuichi*. The memoir was rereleased under a few different titles and eventually became a bestseller. In 2017, it was turned into a movie called *Jungle* starring Daniel Radcliffe.

As for Ruprechter and Stamm, they never made it out of the jungle. Both Ghinsberg and Gale looked for them after finally making it to safety. But their search came up empty. There were no records of two backpackers fitting their description ever reaching Apolo, La Paz, or any other place near the Bolivian Amazon. Their bodies were never found.

CULTURAL IMPACT
ECOTOURISM IN MADIDI

Ten years after his ordeal, Yossi Ghinsberg returned to San José de Uchupiamonas. The villagers told him that they dreamed of building a place that would encourage more visitors to travel to the region. A lodge would provide much-needed employment opportunities for the people.

Ghinsberg asked some organizations for donations. From 1992 to 1995, he lived in the community and helped with the project. In 1995, Chalalán Ecolodge—Bolivia's first ecolodge, a tourist accommodation with little impact on the environment—opened in Madidi National Park. With open-air cabins on stilts, Chalalán became a place where people could listen to the sounds of macaws and howler monkeys as they gazed out at the jungle.

▲ Open-air cabins have screens rather than glass windows so air can flow freely.

In 2017, the lodge employed 120 local families. After the film *Jungle* was released, Ghinsberg hoped the film would drive even more tourism to the area. "My highest aspiration [is that it] will drive a renewed attention to this remote part of the world, the Madidi," he said. "It is where the story not only took place but also still unfolds."[6]

CHAPTER 7

FOUND ALIVE AFTER 17 DAYS

When 35-year-old Amanda Eller woke up on May 8, 2019, she was sure of one thing: she wanted to go for a nice, relaxing walk in the woods. Ever since she had moved to Maui, a Hawaiian island, she had done a lot of exploring. She loved being able to just walk out the door or go for a drive and be surrounded by beautiful nature.

That morning, Eller decided to go to the Makawao Forest Reserve, an area of protected woodlands in northern Maui that is full of massive kupukupu ferns and rainbow eucalyptus trees. It is hilly and has several trails. She hadn't been to that park in months and

◀ The dense canopy in forests such as Makawao Forest Reserve make it nearly impossible to spot people in them from the air.

was looking forward to some peace and tranquility. She drove to one of the major trails in the reserve, intending to take a short hike. The day's temperatures were warming up, and there was a possibility of rain. But as a yoga instructor and physical therapist, Eller knew she could handle the three-mile (4.8 km) trail.[1] She wore a tank top and capri-length leggings to stay cool.

Before she started on the hike, Eller thought about bringing her phone with her on the hike. But because she thought she'd be gone only a short period of time and had done the hike before, she decided to leave her phone in her locked car. She also left behind her wallet and water bottle so she wouldn't have to carry additional weight on the trail. It turned out to be one of the biggest mistakes of her life.

TURNED AROUND

A short while into her hike, Eller wandered off the path to find a place to rest. She wanted to spend a few minutes meditating on all the beauty around her. But the quick pit stop became a turning point in an adventure she would not soon forget. When she tried to get back to the trail, Eller realized she didn't know where it was. No matter how hard she looked, she couldn't find her bearings.

"I laid down on a tree and I was looking at the sky and when I got up and I tried to go back the way that I came, which I had a sense of direction at that point, the path was not leading me back to my car," Eller said. "And I tried all these different paths and then I was like 'oh shoot, these are not bike paths, these are not walking paths, these are boar paths.'"[2]

Without a better plan, Eller did the next best thing in her mind: she guessed. That first day, she hiked from 10:30 a.m. until around midnight looking for a footpath that would lead her to her car. "I heard this voice that said, 'If you want to live, keep going,'" she said. "And as soon as I would doubt my intuition and try to go another way than where it was telling me, something would stop

HIKING DOS AND DON'TS

According to hiking experts, there are many things people should always do before heading out on an adventure, including researching the trail before leaving, bringing enough food and water, wearing shoes with sufficient support and traction, and bringing along a cell phone. One thing that many hikers do, even though they shouldn't, is go off-trail. It not only damages vegetation in the area and causes erosion but also increases the chances of getting lost. According to a study done by officials at Great Smoky Mountains National Park, wandering off-trail is the number one reason that adult hikers require rescue—more than injury, instances of bad weather, and loss or failure of equipment combined.

me, a branch would fall on me, I'd stub my toe, or I'd trip. So, I was like, 'O.K., there is only one way to go.'"[3]

Eller tried not to panic. She hiked down steep ravines and through the rich, leafy forest looking for some sign of the trail. She never found her car.

THE GOING GETS TOUGHER

After days of walking and not finding a trail, Eller began to lose hope she'd make it out of the forest alive. She hadn't brought any food or water on the hike, so she had been drinking water out of streams and foraging for anything edible she came across. She picked wild raspberries and strawberry guavas when she could find them. She even ate moths that landed on her arms and legs just to get some protein.

At night, Eller covered herself in fern leaves, wet dirt, moss, and whatever else she could dig up from the ground to stay warm. One night, she even slept in a boar's den, hoping she wouldn't be discovered. Temperatures dropped to around 60 degrees Fahrenheit (16°C) in the evening, so she wasn't at risk of frostbite or hypothermia.[4] The cool mist and frequent rain washed away her sweat and kept the bugs from bothering her.

▲ Strawberry guava plants were brought to Hawaii in the early 1800s, but they began spreading in the wild and are now invasive in Hawaii.

▲ People who get lost in a forest on Maui have many hills and streams that they need to navigate.

Still, the going wasn't easy. She fell 20 feet (6 m) off a cliff, fracturing one of her legs and tearing some cartilage in her knee.[5] She also lost her shoes in a flash flood and was forced to continue barefoot. She began to crawl instead of walk. Every time she heard a helicopter overhead, she flailed her arms and yelled into the sky, but the canopy was so dense that no one could see her. After what seemed like an endless amount of time, Eller was sure she had to be getting closer to her car. What she didn't realize was that she was going deeper and deeper into the forest.

MAUI MOBILIZES

As Eller's ordeal ran into the second week, she began to lose hope. But little did she know that a massive rescue mission was underway. On May 9, her boyfriend had reported her missing. Eller's parents also got involved in the search. After local

DANGERS OF FLASH FLOODS IN HAWAII

It rains a lot in the Hawaiian Islands. Therefore, flash floods are possible at any time of the year. They are most frequent during the Hawaiian wet season, which extends from October through April. Flash floods are one of the leading causes of weather-related deaths in the state. An average of 11 flash floods happen every year on the islands.[6] When a flood might occur, the National Weather Service issues a warning to the public to prepare for the threat.

▲ Various kinds of technology, including drones, were used in the search for Eller.

authorities found Eller's abandoned car at the trailhead, police and firefighters scoured the perimeter of the reserve for any signs that Eller had been there.

Seventy-two hours after Eller disappeared, Maui officials stopped searching for her, believing it was a lost cause.

But hundreds of local volunteers and some search and rescue dogs took over in their place. They scoured the park for clothing, footprints, and anything else that might give them a clue about Eller's whereabouts. Some rappelled into canyons and dived into swirling pools of water. Others looked inside caves and waded through swift-moving streams. At least one person was attacked by a wild boar during the search. For days, their efforts came up empty.

On the seventeenth day, growing continually more concerned, Eller's parents issued a $50,000 reward for anyone who had information about their daughter's whereabouts.[7] Just a few hours later, a helicopter happened to spot Eller in a deep ravine. Looking up from below, Eller couldn't believe what she saw.

"I'm seeing these guys come over me in a helicopter and I can't tell you, like, my heart just fell through my feet," Eller said. "I mean I just

WILD BOARS

Though wild boars look similar to farm pigs, they are quite different from their domestic counterparts. They are covered in coarse brown or gray fur and have very large heads for the size of their bodies. Males have sharp tusks that extend from their mouths. They can run at speeds of up to 25 miles per hour (40 kmh).[8] Some wild boars will attack humans in self-defense, if they feel cornered, or to protect their young. The best way for people to protect themselves against wild boars is to back away slowly and get to higher ground than the animal.

collapsed. I had a plant in my mouth that I was planning on eating for dinner."[9]

Javier Cantellops, a search coordinator and former Army Ranger who was in the helicopter, spotted Eller by a stream at the bottom of a deep gulch. It was seven miles (11 km) by air from the area around the trailhead where the other volunteers were looking. That's about 30 miles (48 km) on foot, factoring in the rise and fall of the ground.[10]

The helicopter dropped three members of a search and rescue team—Cantellops, Chris Berquist, and Troy Helmer—by the creek. When the team reached her, Eller broke down in tears. Cantellops said it was the best moment of his life.

After making sure she didn't have any life-threatening injuries, the rescuers secured Eller onto a gurney. Then she was airlifted to an airport and flown to a hospital. Her feet were swollen and in terrible shape. She had serious sunburn and a skin infection, and she had lost 15 pounds (6.8 kg).[11] But she was alive.

> **There were times of total fear and loss and wanting to give up. It did come down to life and death and I had to choose. I chose life—I wasn't going to take the easy way out.[12]**
>
> *—Amanda Eller, in a Facebook video post after she was rescued, 2019*

▲ *From left*, Javier Cantellops, Amanda Eller, Troy Helmer, and Chris Berquist took a photo together shortly after the three rescuers found Eller.

"I have the most gratitude and respect and appreciation. I can't even put it into words for the people who helped me," Eller said in a video she posted on Facebook after she was rescued. "The last 17 days of my life have been the toughest days of my life."[13]

CHAPTER 8

SURVIVING THE FOREST AND JUNGLE

Getting stranded or lost in the jungle or forest is a harrowing ordeal. Everyone should be careful when traveling through these areas. Whether it's making a home near a forest or jungle environment, camping in it, kayaking through it, or just going for a hike, there are a number of precautions people should take to ensure they're fully prepared.

Before any excursion into the forest or jungle, it's a good idea to check the weather forecast, find out about trail closures or wildfire risks, and become familiar with the topography and ecology of the region to be best prepared for any emergency. A compass

◀ There are many precautions people can take to help them survive if they ever do get lost in a forest.

and topographic map are key to avoid getting lost. For tech-savvy adventurers, a GPS device that can function in areas without cell phone service is especially helpful.

Beyond being aware of the landforms and placement of things such as rivers, streams, caves, and valleys, knowing what to eat and what to avoid is essential to staying alive. If hunting or fishing isn't possible or preferable, surviving on plants is doable. But it can be deadly to eat an unknown plant, so it's best not to do so, even in emergencies.

For hikers, trail runners, and other adventurers, some common tips are to steer clear of yellow or white berries. Foraged mushrooms can also be lethal. While some, such as chanterelles and lobster mushrooms, are safe to eat, there are a lot of look-alikes that are poisonous. People should also stay away from plants with thorns, with umbrella-shaped flowers, or with seeds inside a pod. Many of those, such as poison hemlock, are toxic.

Foods that are safe to eat include coconuts, sugarcane, papayas, taro roots, palm hearts, and figs. Even though it might sound gross, insects such as worms, grubs, and

> *The number one mistake I see is lack of preparation.*[1]
>
> **—Andrew Herrington, ranger in Great Smoky Mountains National Park**

termites are a smart last-resort source of protein. Plants can also be used for first aid in a pinch. Blisters, burns, and cuts can be treated using balsam, subalpine, or Douglas fir sap as an antibacterial resin.

Survival experts recommend staying on the trail at all times and avoiding wandering aimlessly whenever possible. Taking shortcuts on mapped trails is also frowned upon. "There's usually a reason why trails and roads go the way that they do, even with all their seemingly senseless twists,

▼ **Palm hearts are harvested from the center of palm trees just below where the leaves come out.**

turns and switchbacks. These trails are likely avoiding difficult terrain," says survival expert Tim MacWelch. "When people try to find a shortcut off the trail, their bushwhacking often places them in an area where it's easy to get lost. Stick to the designated trails, and you'll likely get there faster—and avoid getting lost."[2]

WEAR THE RIGHT CLOTHING

Wearing the right clothing on a jungle or forest adventure is essential to having a great time without overheating or getting soaked. Lightweight, loose-fitting, moisture-wicking clothes that let air pass through can slow dehydration and provide a barrier against the wind. Stretchy layers make it easier to climb up and down rocky terrain. Because it can rain at any time in the forest and especially in the jungle, waterproof clothing, including a rain jacket, is a must. Long pants and a shirt with long sleeves help guard against poisonous plants and bug stings.

In addition to using sunscreen, many hikers wear clothing with ultraviolet protection factor (UPF) 50 built in, sunglasses, and a wide-brimmed hat. Closed-toe shoes with traction, such as waterproof hiking boots or work boots with heavy-duty tread, are important to keeping the body

▶ FOREST ADVENTURE CHECKLIST

It's important to have a checklist of items to bring before heading out into the forest or jungle. A person's exact checklist will vary based on where they are going and for how long.

CLOTHING AND GEAR

☑ MOSQUITO NET AND HAT ☑ HIKING BOOTS ☑ RAIN GEAR

TOOLS

☑ POCKETKNIFE ☑ GPS ☑ MAP ☑ HEADLAMP

HEALTH AND WELLNESS

☑ BUG SPRAY ☑ FIRST AID KIT ☑ WATERPROOF MATCHES ☑ WATER FILTER

> **IS DEET SAFE?**
>
> Scientists agree that DEET is the most effective bug spray to use to prevent mosquito bites. It repels the insects through its bad taste and smell. Some studies in the past have tied DEET to seizures or brain toxicity in children. Others have suggested that it prevents the body's normal breakdown of acetylcholine, a chemical in the nervous system that sparks movement and muscle activity. But these studies have since been disproven. "There could be bad reactions if it's misused—like if you drink it or breathe it in. But it's safe when used properly," says Jonathan Day, a professor of medical entomology at the University of Florida.[3]

stable on rugged terrain and go a long way in preventing people from sinking in the mud or slipping on wet rocks.

Perhaps the most important piece of clothing is a wearable net for defense against mosquitoes, wasps, biting ants, and other stinging or biting insects that carry disease or cause irritation. Many hats at outdoor stores come with nets attached. There are other nets available with a drawstring that fit over a hat and cinch at the neck to protect the face, ears, and neck.

PACK THE BEST GEAR

After getting an outfit ready, the next step for forest explorers is to pack a waterproof backpack full of helpful gear. Insect repellent with picaridin or DEET should be at the top of every jungle excursion packing list. Natural products such as vitamin B1 skin patches or citronella candles might seem great, but they don't work well against fierce forest or jungle insects. Tablets that help prevent malaria are useful for hikers traveling to forests or jungles where malaria-carrying mosquitoes are present.

Next, the National Park Service recommends that every trekker or explorer should include a repair kit in their pack in case something breaks or they need to build a temporary shelter. The kit should include a multi-tool that can be used to cut up food, rip clothing for a tourniquet after an injury, and defend against wildlife. If there's room, duct tape or rope can be tied to trees in case a makeshift shelter is needed. A flint-and-steel set or waterproof matches are necessary for starting a fire if it's dry enough to do so.

A LifeStraw—a water filter shaped like a straw—an ultraviolet (UV) light, water purification tablets, or another type of water filter is a must-have to prevent waterborne diseases. Each one has its own purpose. UV lights kill pathogens in mostly clear water, but they don't work well on muddy river water. Water purification tablets such as Aquatabs are effective against viruses, bacteria, and giardia, but they don't protect against cryptosporidia, microscopic parasites that cause long-lasting diarrhea. Many outdoor experts consider portable reverse-osmosis water filters to be the best option. They can filter out debris and parasites in addition to viruses and bacteria.

Outdoor safety experts Frank Meyer and Jared Jones recommend putting health and safety tools first when preparing for a forest or jungle adventure. Headlamps or flashlights are key for seeing in the dark. A police-style whistle and a small mirror are great tools to use for signaling

▼ A good hiking backpack can hold everything a person needs for a forest adventure.

and can be heard or seen from miles away. A fold-up reflective Mylar blanket found at outdoor stores can be used as an extra layer or as something to wave in the air to catch a search and rescue helicopter's attention.

First aid kits are also crucial. Gauze, bandages, pain killers, antibiotic ointment, antidiarrheal pills, and blister treatments are just some of the things to include in the kit. Even if it contains only a few supplies, a first aid kit can help reduce minor aches and pains, making the adventure more enjoyable.

Finally, personal locator beacons (PLBs) and satellite phones are critical to have for emergency situations that happen in remote or out-of-cell-range areas. A PLB is a satellite-synced device that sends a signal and the user's location to rescue agencies. With a satellite phone, a stranded person can send out a signal to a local emergency number, send and receive phone calls, and send short text messages. An open view of the sky, not blocked by trees or clouds, is required for a satellite device to work effectively.

STAY HYDRATED

No matter the environment, staying hydrated is paramount to surviving in the wilderness. If it's hot and humid, it's especially important. "A good general recommendation is about one half-liter [17 ounces] of water per hour of moderate activity in moderate temperatures," say REI instructor Megan Stump and wilderness medicine expert Gates Richards. "You may need to increase how much you drink as the temperature and intensity of the activity rise."[4]

But running out of water isn't a death sentence. In forests and jungles, there are many places to find it. In jungles, bamboo stalks and thick vines that wrap around trees store water inside. The thicker the vine, the more liquid it holds, though it's important to know which vines produce poisonous sap. Leaves from other large plants can be used as funnels to collect rainwater or even as storage containers if they are big enough. For drinking, river or stream water should always

CREATE A SOLAR STILL

One way to collect water in the jungle is to create a solar still. The first step is digging a hole in a sunny area that's about three feet (0.9 m) wide and two feet (0.6 m) deep, with a smaller indent in the center.[5] Next is placing a wide-mouthed bottle, a large cupped leaf, or another container in the indent. The third step is laying a piece of plastic over the hole and lining the edge with rocks so it stays in place. Putting one small rock in the center of the piece of plastic creates an inverted cone. The sun's heat will cause moisture from the ground to evaporate. The evaporated moisture will accumulate underneath the plastic and drip down the cone into the container.

▲ People heading into the forest with a pet must bring items such as water and food for the pet in addition to their own supplies.

be boiled or filtered so it's free of any harmful contaminants, animal urine, or waterborne diseases. Anytime people engage in physical activity, it's important to drink before feeling thirsty to prevent dehydration.

LET PEOPLE KNOW

One of the most important things a person can do before embarking on a trip into the jungle or forest is to tell a friend or family member their plans. That includes where they're going, when they will get there, and when they will return. That way, if something bad happens, the family member or friend can alert the authorities, whether it's a park ranger, a search and rescue team, or the police.

If there is an information card at the beginning of the trailhead, hikers can also fill one out. These cards are usually located in a box by the wall maps of the area. Hikers and adventurers should make sure to fill in all the details, most importantly the dates of the excursion. The information on these cards can help hikers be found quickly in an emergency.

WHAT TO DO IN AN EMERGENCY

Many people spend a day, a week, or a month in the forest or jungle and enjoy the experience. But emergencies do happen. The best thing to do is to try to get help in whatever way possible.

When in doubt, lost hikers should follow an animal trail, go downhill, and try to find a water source that will lead out of the forest. Breaking branches at eye level or lining up rocks as a locator for a rescue team is also smart. People should always walk in the day and find shelter to sleep in at night. There are a lot of dangerous animals out after dark. It's wise not to move around and attract attention.

When on an outdoor adventure, hikers should always stay away from large animals such as wild boars, cougars, and bears. Loud noises can provoke an attack, so blending into the environment is crucial. If someone spots a dangerous predator, backing away slowly is recommended. Turning away can make a person look like prey.

Most importantly, thinking clearly whenever possible should be a top priority. Panicking can lead to poor decisions. "I always like to take a deep breath, sit down, eat a snack, drink water, and then pull out all of my available navigation tools: guidebook, map, compass, GPS, etc.," says Jennifer Pharr Davis, owner of the Blue Ridge Hiking Company. "I ask myself where and when I last remember being on the right trail, and then I use my available resources to make a plan."[6] With a clear head, people have the best chance of survival.

THE SMOKY MOUNTAINS

In 2017, 18-year-old Austin Bohanan got lost in the Great Smoky Mountains National Park while on a hike with his stepfather. After spending a chilly night by himself on a ridge, he decided to keep moving. He found a stream and followed it down the mountain. He walked for 11 days without food. Eventually the stream led him to a bigger creek. There, he saw some kayaks and a boat carrying a man and his daughter, who brought him to safety. "The main thing was just keep my calm, keep my cool, just keep moving. It's just instinct, I guess, that came out," he said.[7]

ESSENTIAL FACTS

SURVIVAL STORIES

- Juliane Koepcke was the only survivor of the LANSA Flight 508 plane crash in 1971. She survived 11 days in the Amazon jungle before walking and swimming her way back to civilization.

- Shoichi Yokoi was a Japanese soldier during World War II who fled into Guam's thick jungle when the US military took back control of the island in 1944. Yokoi survived in the jungle for 27 years before he was found and sent back to Japan in 1972.

- Pamela Salant walked away from her boyfriend after an argument while the couple was looking for a campsite in Mount Hood National Forest in 2011. She fell off a ledge, broke her leg, and survived by eating berries before she was located and picked up by a search and rescue team.

- Yossi Ghinsberg got separated from a group of backpackers looking for gold in the Bolivian Amazon in 1981 after careening over a waterfall. For three weeks he wandered around the jungle, battling a jaguar, beating off fire ants, and staving off extreme hunger before being rescued.

- Amanda Eller got lost during a hike in Makawao Forest Reserve on Hawaii's Maui island in 2019. Without her phone, food, or water, she spent the next 17 days fighting for her life in the forest, trying to get back to her car.

FOREST AND JUNGLE SURVIVAL

- A forest is a lush ecosystem populated mostly by trees. Forests can be divided into three main types: boreal, temperate, and tropical (also called jungles).

- Forests cover about one-third of Earth's land surface. About 300 million people live in forests. More than one billion people depend on these areas for their livelihood.

- Some of the main hazards of forests and jungles are waterborne illnesses, poisonous or disease-carrying plants and animals, lightning strikes, falling trees, and flash floods.

- To survive in a forest or jungle, the most important thing to do is to remain calm. Another smart tip is to find a river, which will eventually lead to civilization.

- Other survival tips include wearing a wide-brimmed hat with a mosquito net and closed-toe shoes with traction, like hiking boots.

- A forest or jungle survival kit should include a first aid kit, sunscreen, a loud whistle, mosquito repellent, waterproof matches, and a water filter or water purification tablets.

QUOTE

"The jungle is as much a part of me as my love for my husband, the music of the people who live along the Amazon and its tributaries, and the scars that remain from the plane crash."

—*Juliane Koepcke in an interview with the* New York Times, *June 18, 2021*

GLOSSARY

arachnid
A grouping of invertebrates that have two body segments and four pairs of legs; includes spiders and scorpions.

biodiverse
Having many different plants and animals in an ecosystem.

biome
A community of plants and animals that adapt to and live in a specific climate.

careen
To move quickly in a random, often out-of-control direction.

demoralized
Beaten down emotionally; having lost confidence.

ecosystem
A community of interacting organisms and their environment.

emaciated
Very thin.

fascism
A political system in which the government controls the economy and no opposing political parties are permitted.

gangrene
A serious condition in which the loss of blood supply, such as to a leg or arm, causes the tissue to die.

gurney
A stretcher.

hypothermia
The condition of having an unusually low body temperature, which endangers health.

impenetrable
The state of being impossible to pass through.

infestation
The presence of a massive number of pests, such as insects, in an area, potentially causing serious damage or disease.

midlatitudes
The temperate zone latitudes from 30 to 60 degrees north or south of the equator.

negligence
Failure to take proper care in doing something.

perilous
Dangerous or very risky.

rappel
To lower oneself down a mountain or rock face using a harness and climbing rope.

reservoir
A human-made lake for storing water for people to use.

secrete
To form and release a substance.

strenuous
Requiring great energy or effort.

suture
To stitch up a wound.

topography
The arrangement of physical features of a landscape, including mountains, hills, and rivers.

zoologist
A scientist who studies animals and how they interact with their environment.

ADDITIONAL RESOURCES

SELECTED BIBLIOGRAPHY

Burnett, Derek. "Nightmare in the Woods." *Reader's Digest*, 14 Feb. 2023, rd.com. Accessed 24 Apr. 2023.

Kelly, Stephen R. "How a Long-Lost Soldier's Survival Story Riveted—and Confounded—'70s Japan." *Slate*, 31 Jan. 2022, slate.com. Accessed 24 Apr. 2023.

Kerr, Breena. "Amanda Eller, Hiker Lost in Hawaii Forest, Is Found Alive after 17 Days." *New York Times*, 25 May 2019, nytimes.com. Accessed 24 Apr. 2023.

FURTHER READINGS

Pelleschi, Andrea. *Amazon Explorers*. Abdo, 2020.

Sonneborn, Liz. *Rock and Mountain Survival Stories*. Abdo, 2024.

Towell, Colin. *The Survival Handbook: Essential Skills for Outdoor Adventure*. DK, 2020.

ONLINE RESOURCES

To learn more about forests, jungles, and survival, please visit **abdobooklinks.com** or scan this QR code. These links are routinely monitored and updated to provide the most current information available.

MORE INFORMATION

For more information on this subject, contact or visit the following organizations:

CHALALÁN ECOLODGE
Comercio St.
Rurrenabaque, Bolivia
info@chalalan.com
chalalan.com/en/

Chalalán Ecolodge is the lodge Yossi Ghinsberg helped construct in Madidi National Park. Visitors can stay at the lodge. They can also book guided tours into the Bolivian jungle, talk with members of the community, and witness jungle animals in their natural habitat.

MOUNT HOOD CULTURAL CENTER AND MUSEUM
88900 Government Camp Loop
Government Camp, OR 97028
info@mthoodmuseum.org
mthoodmuseum.org/

Mount Hood Cultural Center and Museum serves as the information center for Mount Hood National Park. It features interactive exhibits, a gallery for local artists, and a gift shop. Tourists can find out about popular trails, ski on the mountain, learn safety precautions, and talk to park stewards.

PANGUANA
info@panguana.com
https://panguana.de/?lang=en

Panguana is the biological research station Juliane Koepcke's parents started in 1968 that is still running today. Here and on the center's website, visitors can find out more about the plants and animals that live in the Peruvian Amazon and the current conservation projects to protect and preserve them.

SOURCE NOTES

CHAPTER 1. PLUMMETING FROM THE SKY

1. Franz Lidz. "She Fell Nearly 2 Miles, and Walked Away." *New York Times*, 18 June 2021, nytimes.com. Accessed 12 July 2023.
2. "Home Page." *Panguana*, n.d., panguana.de. Accessed 12 July 2023.
3. Katherine Macdonald. "Survival Stories: The Girl Who Fell from the Sky." *Reader's Digest*, 1 Mar. 2023, rd.com. Accessed 12 July 2023.
4. Rebecca Armitage. "How Teenager Juliane Koepcke Survived a Plane Crash and Solo 11-Day Trek out of the Amazon." *ABC News*, 1 Oct. 2022, abc.net.au. Accessed 12 July 2023.
5. "Lightning and Planes." *National Weather Service*, n.d., weather.gov. Accessed 12 July 2023.
6. Lidz, "She Fell Nearly 2 Miles."
7. Macdonald, "Survival Stories."
8. Rhett A. Butler. "The Amazon Rainforest: The World's Largest Rainforest." *Mongabay*, 4 June 2020, rainforests.mongabay.com. Accessed 12 July 2023.
9. Tim MacWelch. "10 Reasons People Get Lost in the Wild." *Outdoor Life*, 20 Apr. 2021, outdoorlife.com. Accessed 12 July 2023.
10. MacWelch, "10 Reasons People Get Lost."

CHAPTER 2. DANGERS OF THE FOREST AND JUNGLE

1. *Our Forests and Jungles*. Our Planet Netflix and World Wildlife Fund, n.d., panda.org. Accessed 12 July 2023.
2. *Our Forests and Jungles*.
3. Katherine Gallagher. "10 Largest and Most Biodiverse Forests on Earth." *Treehugger*, 20 Sept. 2022, treehugger.com. Accessed 12 July 2023.
4. Lee J. T. White, et al. "Congo Basin Rainforest—Invest US$150 Million in Science." *Nature*, vol. 595, 2021, pp. 411–414, nature.com. Accessed 24 July 2023.
5. Anna Nordseth. "Types of Forests: Definitions, Examples, and Importance." *Treehugger*, 30 Nov. 2022, treehugger.com. Accessed 12 July 2023.
6. Nordseth, "Types of Forests."
7. "Forest Biome." *National Geographic Education*, 20 May 2022, education.nationalgeographic.org. Accessed 12 July 2023.
8. Nordseth, "Types of Forests."
9. Charles W. Bryant. "How to Survive in the Jungle." *MapQuest Travel*, n.d., mapquest.com. Accessed 12 July 2023.
10. Heather J. Johnson. "Rainforest." *National Geographic Education*, 16 May 2023, education.nationalgeographic.org. Accessed 12 July 2023.
11. "What Animals Live in the Amazon? And 8 Other Amazon Facts." *World Wildlife Fund*, n.d., worldwildlife.org. Accessed 12 July 2023.
12. "Managing Fire." *US Department of Agriculture Forest Service*, n.d., fs.usda.gov. Accessed 12 July 2023.
13. Laurel Wamsley. "Judge Orders Boy Who Started Oregon Wildfire to Pay $36 Million in Restitution." *NPR*, 22 May 2018, npr.org. Accessed 12 July 2023.
14. "Malaria." *World Health Organization*, 29 Mar. 2023, who.int. Accessed 12 July 2023.
15. Helen Thompson. "14 Fun Facts about Piranhas." *Smithsonian Magazine*, 8 July 2014, smithsonianmag.com. Accessed 12 July 2023.
16. Oishimaya Sen Nag. "The Most Dangerous Animals of the Amazon Rainforest." *World Atlas*, 1 Aug. 2017, worldatlas.com. Accessed 12 July 2023.
17. Riley Fortier. "5 of the Most Poisonous Tropical Rainforest Plants." *PlantSnap*, 24 Aug. 2020, plantsnap.com. Accessed 12 July 2023.

CHAPTER 3. A PATH OUT OF THE JUNGLE

1. Katherine Macdonald. "Survival Stories: The Girl Who Fell from the Sky." *Reader's Digest*, 1 Mar. 2023, rd.com. Accessed 12 July 2023.
2. Franz Lidz. "She Fell Nearly 2 Miles, and Walked Away." *New York Times*, 18 June 2021, nytimes.com. Accessed 12 July 2023.
3. Lidz, "She Fell Nearly 2 Miles."
4. "Juliane Koepcke: How I Survived a Plane Crash." *BBC News*, 24 Mar. 2012, bbc.com. Accessed 12 July 2023.
5. Rebecca Armitage. "How Teenager Juliane Koepcke Survived a Plane Crash and Solo 11-Day Trek out of the Amazon." *ABC News*, 1 Oct. 2022, abc.net.au. Accessed 12 July 2023.
6. Macdonald, "Survival Stories."
7. Lidz, "She Fell Nearly 2 Miles."
8. Lidz, "She Fell Nearly 2 Miles."
9. Lidz, "She Fell Nearly 2 Miles."

CHAPTER 4. TWENTY-SEVEN YEARS IN HIDING

1. David Vergun. "Nation Observes 80th Anniversary of Attack on Pearl Harbor." *US Department of Defense*, 7 Dec. 2021, defense.gov. Accessed 12 July 2023.
2. Sydney Combs. "In WWII, the Japanese Invaded Guam. Now They're Welcomed as Tourists." *National Geographic*, 13 Dec. 2019, nationalgeographic.com. Accessed 12 July 2023.
3. Combs, "The Japanese Invaded Guam."
4. Nicholas D. Kristof. "Shoichi Yokoi, 82, Is Dead; Japan Soldier Hid 27 Years." *New York Times*, 26 Sept. 1997, nytimes.com. Accessed 12 July 2023.
5. Meilan Solly. "The Japanese WWII Soldier Who Refused to Surrender for 27 Years." *Smithsonian Magazine*, 21 Jan. 2022, smithsonianmag.com. Accessed 12 July 2023.
6. Mike McRae. "Guam's Plague of Snakes Is Devastating the Whole Island Ecosystem, Even the Trees." *ScienceAlert*, 9 Mar. 2017, sciencealert.com. Accessed 12 July 2023.
7. Solly, "Japanese WWII Soldier."
8. Stephen R. Kelly. "How a Long-Lost Soldier's Survival Story Riveted—and Confounded—'70s Japan." *Slate*, 31 Jan. 2022, slate.com. Accessed 12 July 2023.
9. Dominica Tolentino. "WWII: Sgt. Shoichi Yokoi, Last Straggler on Guam." *Guampedia*, 11 Apr. 2023, guampedia.com. Accessed 12 July 2023.
10. Tony Pettinato. "WWII Japanese Soldier Surrenders 27 Years after War's End!" *GenealogyBank*, 24 Jan. 2018, blog.genealogybank.com. Accessed 12 July 2023.
11. Kelly, "Long-Lost Soldier's Survival Story."
12. Solly, "Japanese WWII Soldier."
13. Kelly, "Long-Lost Soldier's Survival Story."
14. Kristof, "Shoichi Yokoi, 82, Is Dead."

SOURCE NOTES CONTINUED

CHAPTER 5. A CAMPING TRIP GONE WRONG

1. "Mt. Hood National Forest." *US Department of Agriculture Forest Service*, n.d., fs.usda.gov. Accessed 12 July 2023.
2. "Mount Hood National Forest." *Oregon Wild*, n.d., oregonwild.org. Accessed 12 July 2023.
3. Michael Inbar. "She Survived Four Days in Wilderness Eating Bugs, Slugs." *Today*, 9 Apr. 2011, today.com. Accessed 12 July 2023.
4. Derek Burnett. "Nightmare in the Woods." *Reader's Digest*, 14 Feb. 2023, rd.com. Accessed 12 July 2023.
5. Burnett, "Nightmare in the Woods."
6. Burnett, "Nightmare in the Woods."
7. Kevin Dolak. "Oregon Hiker Falls 50 Feet, Survived 3 Days on Bugs, Berries." *ABC News*, 8 Aug. 2011, abcnews.go.com. Accessed 12 July 2023.
8. Burnett, "Nightmare in the Woods."
9. Burnett, "Nightmare in the Woods."
10. Burnett, "Nightmare in the Woods."
11. Burnett, "Nightmare in the Woods."

CHAPTER 6. LOST IN THE BOLIVIAN AMAZON

1. "The Real Story behind the Movie *Jungle*—Heroic Survival and Mysterious Disappearances." *StrangeOutdoors*, 1 May 2021, strangeoutdoors.com. Accessed 12 July 2023.
2. "Madidi National Park." *Global Alliance of National Parks*, n.d., national-parks.org. Accessed 12 July 2023.
3. "Madidi National Park: Bolivia's Jungle Paradise." *Bolivia Hop*, n.d., boliviahop.com. Accessed 12 July 2023.
4. Simon Round. "I Was Lost in the Amazon Jungle." *Jewish Chronicle*, 24 Nov. 2016, thejc.com. Accessed 12 July 2023.
5. Round, "I Was Lost."
6. Claire Boobbyer. "Will Daniel Radcliffe's *Jungle* Film Help Save Bolivian Ecotourism?" *Adventure.com*, 18 Oct. 2017, adventure.com. Accessed 12 July 2023.

CHAPTER 7. FOUND ALIVE AFTER 17 DAYS

1. Breena Kerr. "Amanda Eller, Hiker Lost in Hawaii Forest, Is Found Alive After 17 Days." *New York Times*, 25 May 2019, nytimes.com. Accessed 12 July 2023.
2. Jonathan Vigliotti. "Maui Hiker Details How She Survived 17 Days in the Jungle." *CBS News*, 28 May 2019, cbsnews.com. Accessed 12 July 2023.
3. Kerr, "Amanda Eller."
4. Kerr, "Amanda Eller."
5. Kerr, "Amanda Eller."
6. "Flood." *City and County of Honolulu Department of Emergency Management*, n.d., honolulu.gov. Accessed 12 July 2023.
7. Kerr, "Amanda Eller."
8. Andreea Stoica. "How to Survive a Wild Boar Attack | All You Need to Know." *Restless Backpacker*, 10 Jan. 2022, restlessbackpacker.com. Accessed 12 July 2023.
9. Vigliotti, "Maui Hiker."
10. Kerr, "Amanda Eller."
11. John Bacon. "'I Chose Life': Hiker Amanda Eller Survived on Wild Fruit, Water, and Grit for 17 Days in the Hawaiian Forest." *USA Today*, 26 May 2019, usatoday.com. Accessed 12 July 2023.
12. Bacon, "'I Chose Life'"
13. Francesca Gariano. "Men Who Found Amanda Eller Share Details on Her 'Unbelievable' Rescue." *Today*, 27 May 2019, today.com. Accessed 12 July 2023.

CHAPTER 8. SURVIVING THE FOREST AND JUNGLE

1. "Safe & Found." *SmokyMountains.com*, n.d., smokymountains.com. Accessed 12 July 2023.
2. Tim MacWelch. "10 Reasons People Get Lost in the Wild." *Outdoor Life*, 20 Apr. 2021, outdoorlife.com. Accessed 12 July 2023.
3. Markham Heid. "DEET Is the Most Effective Bug Spray. But Is It Safe?" *Time*, 25 July 2018, time.com. Accessed 12 July 2023.
4. Megan Stump and Gates Richards. "How to Stay Hydrated on the Trail." *REI*, n.d., rei.com. Accessed 12 July 2023.
5. Charles W. Bryant. "How to Find Water in the Wild." *MapQuest Travel*, 9 Apr. 2021, mapquest.com. Accessed 12 July 2023.
6. Derrick Bryson Taylor. "Going Hiking? Don't Forget These Safety Tips." *New York Times*, 29 July 2022, nytimes.com. Accessed 12 July 2023.
7. "Safe & Found."

INDEX

airplanes, 6–8, 28, 33, 37, 64
Amazon, 5–6, 9, 11–12, 16, 20, 27, 37, 63–65, 70, 72
animals, 6, 10–13, 15–20, 22–25, 27–33, 36, 41, 42–43, 57, 65, 68, 69, 77–78, 83, 88–89, 92–93, 98
    mosquitoes, 11, 23–24, 28, 33, 34, 44, 69, 91, 92–93

Back from Tuichi, 72
backpacks, 50, 52, 63, 68, 92
Bear Lake, 49, 52–53, 59
Bolivia, 11, 12, 64–65, 72, 73
boreal forests, 16

camping, 12, 25, 49–53, 61, 63, 87
Chalalán Ecolodge, 73
clothes, 8, 10, 44, 61, 83, 90, 91, 92–93
Colombia, 11, 37, 64
compasses, 52, 87, 99

Eller, Amanda, 12, 75–85
Essig, Aric, 49–52, 57–61

fires, 20–21, 29, 43, 87, 93
first aid, 53, 89, 91, 95
flashlights, 52, 94
floods, 12, 22, 42, 45, 81

food, 17, 19, 29, 37, 42–43, 50, 57–58, 65, 68, 77, 78, 84, 88, 93, 99

Gale, Kevin, 64–65, 67–68, 70–72
Ghinsberg, Yossi, 12, 63–72, 73
GPS, 88, 91, 99
Great Smoky Mountains National Park, 77, 88, 99
Guam, 40–41, 43, 45–47

Hawaii, 12, 39, 75, 81
helicopters, 9, 56, 58–59, 81, 83–84, 95
hiking, 12–13, 37, 49–52, 54, 57, 59, 61, 65, 69, 76–78, 87–88, 90, 91, 93, 98–99

Indigenous people, 37, 64, 65, 68, 70–71
    Witoto people, 37
injuries, 9, 11–12, 25, 53–57, 59, 61, 69, 77, 81, 84, 93
insect repellent, 69, 92

Jungle, 72, 73

Koepcke, Juliane, 5–11, 27–37

MacWelch, Tim, 13, 90
Madidi National Park, 65, 73

Makawao Forest Reserve, 12, 75
maps, 47, 52, 54, 88–89, 91, 98–99
Mount Hood, 12, 49, 50, 56, 57, 59
myiasis, 34

Panguana, 5, 6, 36
Peru, 5, 6, 7, 9, 10, 11, 27, 34
plants, 12, 16–17, 20–22, 24–25, 28–29, 41, 43–45, 53, 56, 78, 84, 88–90, 96
    fruits, 17, 25, 29, 37, 50, 57–58, 68, 78, 88
    trees, 9, 15, 17, 18–19, 21, 24–25, 28–29, 36, 41, 42, 44, 50, 53, 56, 58–59, 68, 75, 77, 89, 93, 95–96

rain, 10, 18–19, 28, 29, 42, 50, 69, 76, 78, 81, 90, 96
rivers, 5, 6, 10, 15, 21, 28, 31–33, 42, 44, 45, 50, 54, 57, 59, 64, 66–67, 68, 70, 72, 88, 93, 96
Ruprechter, Karl, 64–67, 72

Salant, Pamela, 12–13, 49–61
San José de Uchupiamonas, 70, 72, 73

search and rescue, 37, 58, 71–72, 83–84, 95, 97
    Hood River Crag Rats, 59–61
solar stills, 96
Stamm, Marcus, 64–67, 72

temperate forests, 16–19, 28, 49, 50
temperatures, 16–17, 19, 76, 78, 96
trails, 12–13, 21, 49–52, 56–57, 75–76, 77, 78, 82, 84, 87–90, 98–99
trench foot, 25, 66

water, 22–23, 25, 28–29, 31–34, 41, 43, 52–56, 65–67, 68, 69, 76, 77, 78, 83, 96, 98–99
    filters, 50, 91, 93–94, 97
waterfalls, 12, 54, 59, 67–68
When I Fell from the Sky: The True Story of One Woman's Miraculous Survival, 36
World War II, 39–41, 45

Yokoi, Shoichi, 40, 41–47
Yokoi's War and Life on Guam, 1944–1972, 47

ABOUT THE AUTHOR

ALEXIS BURLING

Alexis Burling has written dozens of articles and books for young readers on a variety of topics ranging from current events and biographies of famous people to nutrition, fitness, careers, and money management. She is also a professional book critic with reviews of adult and young adult books, author interviews, and other publishing industry–related articles published in the *New York Times*, *Washington Post Book World*, *San Francisco Chronicle*, and more. Alexis has had the pleasure of hiking and backpacking in many beautiful forests and jungles in the world, including Oregon's Mount Hood National Forest and Madidi National Park in Bolivia. Thankfully she was prepared and didn't get lost. She lives in White Salmon, Washington, with her husband and cats.